Living Liturgies

Published by
The Bible Reading Fellowship
15 The Chambers, Vineyard
Abingdon OX14 3FE
United Kingdom
Tel: +44 (0)1865 319700
Email: enquiries@brf.org.uk
Website: www.brf.org.uk
BRF is a Registered Charity

ISBN 978 0 85746 323 4

First published 2015

10 9 8 7 6 5 4 3 2 1 0

Acknowledgements
Unless otherwise stated, scripture quotations from The New Revised Standard Version of the Bible, Anglicised edition, copyright © 1989, 1995 by the Division of Christian Education of the National Council of the Churches of Christ in the United States of America. Used by permission. All rights reserved.

Scripture taken from *The Message*. Copyright © 1993, 1994, 1995, 1996, 2000, 2001, 2002. Used by permission of NavPress Publishing Group.

Common Worship: Services and Prayers for the Church of England, material from which is included in this service, is copyright © The Archbishop's Council 2000.

Extracts from The Book of Common Prayer of 1662, the rights of which are vested in the Crown in perpetuity within the United Kingdom, are reproduced by permission of Cambridge University Press, Her Majesty's Printers.

Cover photo: Shannon Fagan/The Image bank/Gettyimages

A catalogue record for this book is available from the British Library

Printed and bound by CPI Group (UK) Ltd, Croydon CR0 4YY

Living Liturgies

Transition time resources for services, prayer and conversation with older people

Caroline George

For William, my ever supportive and loving husband, who brought laughter and carnations to the sages of the St Peter's Women's Fellowship.

Acknowledgements

Many, many thanks to the saints of patience and encouragement at Bible Reading Fellowship, including Naomi, Lisa, Karen, Kevin and Debbie.

My gratitude to the priests of St Peter's Church, Hall Green, Birmingham, particularly the Revd Canon Martin Stephenson, who nurtured lay and ordained ministry.

Most of all, my appreciation of the inspirational sages of St Peter's Women's Fellowship.

Contents

Foreword

The best worship ideas are ones which have touched our own hearts first. Those of us responsible for delivering services in care homes, week in, week out, do need a helping hand sometimes when it comes to finding fresh ways of engaging the older people in our impromptu congregations.

Here we have an abundance of tried-and-tested service plans. I like the way Caroline uses everyday objects as themes for liturgies and builds on them. I've lost count of the number of ministers who've said to me, 'What I really need is good ideas for worship, especially with older people', and that applies whether worship is for those in care or still in the community, or those, perhaps, living with dementia. Well, here's the answer to their prayer.

A second-hand idea doesn't mean any diminution of quality. Caroline knows what she is doing because she has been at it a long time, and her experience shines through. The use of items that any one of us has at home as a spring-board for worship emphasises the sacramental nature of the tangible things we take for granted. Like the best worship, they help open our eyes both to what is 'beyond' and what is right in our midst.

Debbie Thrower
Team Leader of The Gift of Years and Anna Chaplain to Older People *(see page 128 for further information)*

Introduction

It was a simple question: 'I think you are just the person. Any chance of popping in to the Women's Fellowship group on Thursday afternoon? They have a devotional service once a month. You know the kind of thing—a couple of hymns, a reading and a few prayers. I know you will enjoy doing it; thanks ever so.'

I smiled and nodded and thought the challenge could be interesting. It was only for one service, after all. Life was busy so I scribbled a few ideas on a postcard, prayed desperately, adapted the ideas as I went along and, through the grace of the Holy Spirit, all was well. The group were generous in their response and asked if I would go again—and so it continued for ten years.

Living Liturgies evolved from my time spent with this group—the St Peter's Women's Fellowship in Hall Green, Birmingham—whose members had accompanied one another in worship and fellowship for many years. I became their worship leader in 1996, as they reached their seventh, eighth and ninth decades of life. They were often described by the wider church community as a group of 'senior citizens', 'elderly people' or 'retired', yet none of these titles did them justice. They were women with a vast combined life experience; given the opportunity to express insight from their personal stories, they had much to share and were inspirational in their determination to continue living the gift of fullness of life with a strong trust and faith in God. The word 'sage',[1] meaning 'a person of great wisdom', would be more appropriate.

The process of ageing is now a popular subject, researched and discussed in political, medical and theological arenas and made visible through the media. In Britain we are constantly being informed of statistics that reveal the increasing number of elderly people within society, resulting from the early years of the Baby Boom plus improved standards of living and advances in health care. The focus of attention is often on the burdens created in the 'fourth age' of life through dependency, lack of finance, the problems of finding appropriate and high-quality care, and the scandal of 'care' provision without dignity and compassion. There is a more positive perception of the activity and presence of people within the 'third age' of life, as the media occasionally acknowledge the significant and integral role played by grandparents in child care, and the extensive contribution of elderly people in the voluntary sector. However, the period of transition from third to fourth age, from independent to dependent living, is, to my knowledge, rarely given attention.

Ageing is a vastly differing experience for each individual: the transition from daily activity within wider society to separation and various degrees of isolation occurs at different ages in different stages and is dependent upon many circumstances. The often-heard comment from friends and family, 'In retrospect, I wish I had [done such-and-such] when s/he was at home or in better health', speaks of a need to share and reflect on the experience of transition. Those who can share experiences in this way may offer significant support and hope for others.

It is heartening to see that much more information is now being aired and shared. This development is visible in the increasing number of books that have emerged during the last two decades, particularly from Christian quarters, covering the subjects of ageing and spirituality, the spiritual care of those with dementia, and death and bereavement. Theological and biblical reflection sit alongside stories of ageing, a good example being Albert Jewell's work, *Ageing, Spirituality and Well-being*. This book includes a powerful chapter by Penelope Wilcock entitled 'The caged bird', which speaks of the experiences of a stroke victim and gives a powerful insight into the reality of life with this condition.[2] James Woodward's *Valuing Age*[3] presents narratives from older adults to inform engagement—a vital ingredient for helpful transition.

As more is published, more questions emerge: there are resources that focus on the condition of dementia, offering guidance and comfort to all parties involved, but I have yet to discover insights into worship and spiritual companionship for those with the lower-profile conditions of Parkinson's disease, motor neurone disease or multiple sclerosis. What do Christians in these circumstances long for in terms of prayer and worship as they journey into dependence?

Christian ministry, both lay and ordained, brings a wealth of experience that continues to be gathered but is not always easily accessible to people who suddenly find themselves with a service to lead or a pastoral visit to make in an unfamiliar context. Elderly people with defined mental or physical conditions, or those who have simply become frail, are in a borderland of transition between the land of the active elderly and the land of those who have become confined within residential walls. Therefore, they require a different response. Statistics from Kate Read, stating that '99% of people over 65 years do not have dementia, and even in the oldest cohorts three–quarters do not have dementia',[4] reveal the need for carefully prepared worship that is relevant and challenging to those whose bodies are frail but who wish to engage and participate in worshipping God. It is this need that has prompted the liturgies and reflections provided in the following pages.

There are many older adults attending and actively participating in Sunday worship and fellowship, but there comes a point when the need for transition from independent living to a more dependent lifestyle makes it difficult for them to take their place in the body of the church on a Sunday. They are often visible within weekday groups, including Women's Fellowship and Mothers' Union meetings, but they are no longer present at Sunday worship. There may be a host of reasons for this absence, including inconvenient service times, problems in the church related to heating and hearing, and the issue of transport. Meanwhile, the weekday groups become, to all intents and purposes, an expression of midweek church, offering an opportunity for the development of creative liturgy and, in particular, transitional liturgy.

The St Peter's Women's Fellowship (which I began to lead), was one such group, whose membership included feisty octogenarians and nonagenarians meeting weekly, with a devotional service at the beginning of each month. Although the members were predominantly women, a few men occasionally attended. Their service was held for many years in the formality of the church's Lady Chapel, followed by tea in another building. As the group members became frail and the journey arduous, it was decided that the service and refreshments would be enjoyed together in the coffee lounge of the church hall.

The move to the coffee lounge led to a change in attitude

towards worship: it was as if the group's perception of and response to church worship had been liberated. Whereas they had gathered in silence in the Lady Chapel, conversation now began before the service and crept into the service itself. There was an unexpected spiritual development. Questions were asked that would not have been asked in the confines of the chapel; comments were made and worship became far more participatory. There was a sense of a natural encounter with the divine through prayer, conversation and scripture. Trevor Dennis describes the encounter and dialogue between God and Adam and Eve in this way: 'It seems so very straightforward, that it does not occur to us to call it prayer on the man and woman's part… Could it be that here, most unusually, we have prayer presented, without any of the usual formalities, simply as conversation? Is this what prayer in Eden is like?'[5] There were many afternoons when, through our conversation, it felt as if we had unexpectedly stumbled across Eden.

The Women's Fellowship devotional services had been a time of connection for the group, creating a link to God in Christ and the Holy Spirit, and connecting members to worship they had participated in throughout their lives. Atkins expresses the active relationship that is created in worship: 'Worship can provide the links we need to be in touch again with the foundations of our relationship with God. Through worship our memories will quickly recapture the relationship at the point where we were last conscious of its importance for us.' He goes on to say, in words that relate to times of transition:

> *Worship assists us to see the present situation in relation to the past and to the future. Worshippers can often be overwhelmed by*

the circumstances of the present. By entering into worship we can link up with the support and guidance we have received from God in the past and feel affirmation in the current situation.[6]

Although the group became far more relaxed in the coffee lounge, allowing for a helpful informality, there remained a need for structured worship that related not only to the group's worship in the Lady Chapel but to their lifetime's experience of worship, whether occasional or on a weekly basis. The devotional services had followed a pattern of hymns, prayers, readings and blessing—a condensed version of an Anglican Service of the Word—without a service sheet but always including the prayer that they had adopted as their Women's Fellowship prayer and the traditional version of the Lord's Prayer.

As the liturgies in this book developed, that structure was retained, but with the addition of opening conversation that could be woven into prayers, visual aids that could be seen easily and times for silent reflection that developed comfortably. Each liturgy was based on a theme, which wove together experience, scripture and the assurance of God's love and grace. For example, the liturgy entitled 'From fire to radiators' offered an opportunity to remember the warmth and activity of life around fires in earlier years, and made a connection to the lakeside fire where the warmth of Jesus' forgiving love was made known to Peter after the resurrection. The prayer time included the idea of bringing to God the ashes of our discomfort and pain, and the flames of our anxieties about ageing and dying. We then received the assurance of the inextinguishable blaze of God's love.

In our preparation for and presentation of worship within the coffee lounge, we needed to move some furniture to create a space that was both practical, allowing ease of vision and hearing, and holy. Chairs were arranged in a circle with a small table as a focal point, usually dressed with a tablecloth, a cross, a candle to be lit at the beginning of the service, and objects or pictures relating to the theme.

We rarely used a service sheet, but participation was enabled by carefully introducing prayer responses or repeated lines of prayer, alongside the use of traditional prayers known by heart. Opening prayers, either before or after conversation, were an integral part of the worship, sometimes including a time of silence or prayers of penitence for all that we had allowed, as individuals and as a society, to separate us from God's love. This was followed by a prayer of absolution. Requests for intercessory prayer were invited and space was made for silent prayer or for individuals to name aloud people or places of concern.

This was the prayer adopted by the group as their Women's Fellowship prayer, always included in their worship.

> O God, make the door of my home wide enough
> to receive all who need human love and friendship;
> narrow enough to shut out all envy, pride and strife.
> Make its threshold smooth enough to be no
> stumbling block to children, nor to straying feet, but
> rugged and strong enough to turn back all evil.
> God, make the door of my home the gateway to
> thine eternal kingdom. Amen[7]

Large-print hymn books were made available and a list of favourite hymns, mostly known by heart, was compiled. CDs were useful aids at times, but the group also loved to sing unaccompanied. There was one afternoon when a member had asked for 'Fight the good fight', but the group knew three different tunes and I thought we might have to call in a mediator to prevent battle commencing! The group also reflected a hidden ecumenism:[8] the members lived locally, and some were included who had previously travelled some distance to attend a church of their own tradition. These members added a fresh dimension to the group in conversation and in their knowledge of different hymns and choruses.

Music played during times of reflection was also enjoyed and often led to familiar hymns and music being recalled.

'Conversation starters', as well as being a way of addressing difficult issues, offered the opportunity for stories to be told, treasured, remembered and brought again to God, connecting personal experience from the past to the present and taking it to the future. It usually took no more than a 'Do you remember?' or 'What was it like when you...?' to set the ball rolling. A careful eye on the time and on more dominant figures, with extra encouragement for quieter members of the group, ensured a balance and flow of conversation within the service.

Bible readings were introduced simply for their connection to the conversation starters and items on the focus table. 'Storytelling' Bible passages and the technique of Godly Play were also effective and were well received by the group, particularly the second time around when the experience had become familiar.

Although each service ended with a blessing or some music, conversation continued as refreshments were served, and only the arrival of lifts home closed the meeting. Worship and fellowship had become completely entwined.

In 2006, the group made the decision to close. New membership had petered out and several stalwarts of the group had died, while others were acknowledging that they were at the point of moving from independent to dependent living and soon would not be able to attend. As the time approached, I spoke with members of the group about the shape and format of the closing services. It was agreed that I should devise a set of services to provide food for thought, making connections to faith in daily life that focused on everyday objects such as windows and tables. These features would remain close at hand, no matter where individuals were, and would be a prompt for prayer.

The composition of the final three liturgies in this book—'Anger and tears' (a service of lament), 'Fragile bones' (a service of healing), and 'Holy journeying' (a closing liturgy) is slightly different, in that they offer more directions and comments for reflection and to facilitate adaption to specific contexts. 'Anger and tears' and 'Fragile bones', though created after the group had closed, reflect the issues that had sometimes created frustration and anger in the group members, as well as their experiences of illness and frailty. A relationship of trust developed over the years, which enabled openness and honesty, in the knowledge that the group was a safe and confidential place to express thoughts and feelings. The final service, 'Holy journeying', was developed around the theme of journeying and affirming the presence of God wherever we travel. It records the worship of the group's final meeting but can also be adapted for a variety of closing contexts.

Using *Living Liturgies*

The opportunity to reflect on my experience with the Women's Fellowship came when I found myself as an ordinand, immersed in theological study, sharing experiences with new colleagues and having access to a wealth of resources in the library at the Queen's Foundation for Ecumenical Theological Education in Birmingham. Thinking back to the time when I started leading the group, it was the memory of my 'busyness', and my awareness of many people in the same predicament who might need resources, that nudged me into recording more fully the liturgies in this book. Although the St Peter's group has closed, all that its members shared and discovered has not been lost; it remains like yeast, ready to act as a raising agent in a variety of contexts.

These liturgies were written for a specific group of British-born white women, who had been part of church communities throughout their lives. However, I believe that they can be easily adapted for mixed gender and multicultural groups, and for worship in day centres or residential homes. Elements could also be used for pastoral time with individuals, or for conversation and reflection with those who have no church affiliation but who wish to express or explore their spirituality.

Our sages may have uncertain futures, particularly if they are facing limitations imposed by frailty. Do elderly people reaching the end of their independent lifestyles feel a little like injured people left at the side of the road? Do they feel spiritually wounded by anxiety, isolation and change? The use of structured conversation within worship creates an opportunity to consider subjects related to ageing that may be avoided in other contexts, thus providing the chance for healing to take place.

The spiritual needs of older people are no less complex than the needs of any other age group, and it is important to be aware of the traditions in which people have participated. There have been change and innovation in worship, new methods of creative teaching and a variety of approaches to prayer in recent decades, but the wider landscape remains and we airbrush it out at the risk of disconnecting our faithful sages. *Living Liturgies* offers the opportunity to include readings and prayers from older adults' lifelong journey of worship, perhaps using the King James Bible, the Book of Common Prayer and other denominational prayer books. Suggestions for hymns and other music, too, may need to reflect your group's familiar favourites.

The use of familiar features at the heart of each service relates to the idea of a memory book or box developed for people with dementia[9] as a spark for conversation and prayer. The features used are also those that will be visible and tangible throughout each day. Transition to a far more isolated lifestyle means that faith connections need to be maintained with church communities, but it is also important to remember the reality of individual needs and the question of how well-equipped individuals are to sustain their faith, when contact with the worshipping community is limited. There must surely be more ways that could be explored, not only to equip people for this period of life but to allow the gift of faith to flourish. *Living Liturgies* offers practical stepping stones for those preparing to enter the fourth age. I hope that you may be able to use these services either as they stand or as an inspiration for developing appropriate services, prayer times or spiritual conversations in your particular context.

As I shared these ideas with friends and colleagues over the years, they requested copies of the liturgies, and then they asked me to add 'something for them'—so I have provided biblical and spiritual reflections at the end of each liturgy, for the benefit of those leading the session. Ministry, whether ordained or lay, is often too busy, and time for reflection may be squeezed out, so I hope that these reflective elements will provide an easy-to-read and user-friendly oasis in the midst of busy preparation. Of course, you may also find that the reflections act as a resource for an introduction or comment after the Bible reading in the liturgy itself.

In your leading of worship for older people, remember that small gestures often make more of an impact than is realised. My husband William occasionally joined us at the Women's Fellowship service. He has a delightful sense of humour and, with just a few words and a carnation for each lady, would lift their spirits and bring a smile to their faces. They always asked, 'When is he coming again?' I don't think he was ever aware of the impact he made: their appreciation of someone who had chosen to be with them, even though he did not have to be, was heartfelt. Invite family or friends to your group from time to time!

Some time after the closure of the St Peter's group, I visited a member in a hospice. She looked from her bed towards the ward window and smiled knowingly at me; then, together, we recalled the Women's Fellowship prayer and the Lord's Prayer and gave thanks to God, her deliverer.

Liturgies

Keys to the door

Arrange a focus table with a candle and a cross (symbols to be used at all services to represent the love and light of Christ) and a bunch or selection of keys.

Welcome and introduction

Today we think about keys and doors, the people who have opened doors for us, doors of opportunity and doors to our faith.

Opening prayers

Introduce the prayer response, 'God be with us: God be with us.'

Lord, open our thoughts
to share the experience of our lives in your presence.
God be with us: **God be with us.**

Lord, open our minds
to listen and see your presence in one another.
God be with us: **God be with us.**

Lord, open our hearts
to know your grace and love at work in our lives.
God be with us: **God be with us. Amen**

Read aloud a traditional prayer or one that is familiar to the group. You might use Hall Green's adaptation of Thomas Ken's prayer, which is particularly appropriate for this service.

O God, make the door of my home wide enough
to receive all who need human love and friendship;
narrow enough to shut out all envy, pride and strife.
Make its threshold smooth enough to be no
stumbling block to children, nor to straying feet,
but rugged and strong enough to turn back all evil.
God, make the door of my home the gateway to
thine eternal kingdom. Amen

Conversation starters

- Who were the people who said to you, 'Have you remembered your keys?'
- Do you have any amusing experiences of forgetting or losing keys?
- Have you ever had responsibility for a set of keys other than for home? How did it feel?
- 'Now you're old enough to have the key of the door.' Was that once a familiar expression when someone reached the age of 21?
- Did you ever hear the expression 'latch-key kids'?
- How did it feel when you had to hand keys back at work or when leaving home?
- What do you think about the saying 'Lock 'em up and throw away the key'? (This conversation starter needs to be used sensitively, with the awareness that there may be offenders or relatives of offenders present.)

- Did family or friends keep the New Year tradition of taking the glowing embers of a fire out of the back door, to represent letting the old year out, and entering through the front door to let the new year in, lighting a new fire for all that was to come? Who carried the embers?
- Who are the people who have opened doors for you, perhaps offering a fresh start or an opportunity that you did not think possible?
- How does it feel to walk through a door for the first time—a new workplace or someone's home?
- Are there doors you don't like to walk through—perhaps the dentist's, the doctor's or the hospital's?
- What does it mean to you to open and close the front door of your own home, and how might it feel if you have to leave your home?
- Have you ever found it difficult to go through the doors of a church?
- Who are the people who have opened the door of faith for you?
- Are there people within the New Testament for whom Jesus opened doors of faith?

Prayers

Use an appropriate prayer book or a 'Kyrie' confession. Introduce the prayer response 'Lord, have mercy' or 'Christ, have mercy.'

You, Lord, know our comings in and our goings out.
Lord, have mercy: **Lord, have mercy.**

You, Lord, know our mistakes and failures.
Christ, have mercy: **Christ, have mercy.**

You, Lord, offer the gift of forgiveness.
Lord, have mercy: **Lord, have mercy.**

May God forgive us, heal and renew us in Christ's name. **Amen**

Hymn suggestions

- Lead us, heav'nly Father, lead us
- Lord, thy word abideth

Take other suggestions from the group.

Bible reading and introduction

Our Bible reading tells of the time when the disciple Peter recognised Jesus as the Messiah and Jesus metaphorically gave him the keys to the kingdom of heaven.

> Now when Jesus came into the district of Caesarea Philippi, he asked his disciples, "Who do people say that the Son of Man is?" And they said, "Some say John the Baptist, but others Elijah, and still others Jeremiah or one of the prophets." He said to them, "But who do you say that I am?" Simon Peter answered, "You are the Messiah, the Son of the living God." And Jesus answered him, "Blessed are you, Simon son of Jonah! For flesh and blood has not revealed this to you, but my Father in heaven. And I tell you, you are Peter, and on this rock I will build my church, and the gates of Hades will not prevail against it. I will give you the keys of the kingdom of heaven, and whatever you bind on earth will be bound in heaven, and whatever you loose

on earth will be loosed in heaven." Then he sternly ordered the disciples not to tell anyone that he was the Messiah.
MATTHEW 16:13–20

Prayers

Ask for prayer requests to weave into the intercessions. Introduce the prayer response 'God, who opens the door of love: hear our prayer.'

We give thanks for people who have unlocked doors to opportunities that have made a difference in our lives: family, friends, colleagues, inspirational people whom we have encountered.
God, who opens the door of love: **hear our prayer.**

As we think of the keys and doors to our homes, we give thanks for home as a place where decisions are made, a place to retreat when life is hard, a place for recalling memories and a place to be in God's presence.
If home has not been an easy place to be, we pray for God to weave a thread of peace into difficult memories.
God, who opens the door of love: **hear our prayer.**

We remember those who have the responsibility of holding prison keys—for staff, for organisations that work with offenders and their families, and for prison chaplains. We pray for all who break laws and commit crimes, that they may turn from all that is wrong and find the key to truth and goodness.
God, who opens the door of love: **hear our prayer.**

As we think of Christ passing the keys of the kingdom to Peter, so we remember those who have unlocked the way of faith for us. We give thanks for the way the word of God has been spoken into our lives. We pray that we in turn will continue to share God's love in our encounters.
God, who opens the door of love: **hear our prayer.**

We think of the ways that we may share our stories of life, our stories of ageing, so that others may be freed to ask questions and to think about ageing and frailty.
God, who opens the door of love: **hear our prayer.**

We give thanks for those we have loved, those who have entered the gates of heaven.

We say together the Lord's Prayer.

Our Father, who art in heaven,
hallowed be thy name;
thy kingdom come;
thy will be done;
in earth as it is in heaven.
Give us this day our daily bread.
And forgive us our trespasses,
as we forgive them that trespass against us.
And lead us not into temptation;
but deliver us from evil.
For thine is the kingdom, the power, and the glory,
for ever and ever. Amen

Closing hymn suggestions

- O praise ye the Lord
- To God be the glory

A blessing

Christ who entered the homes of the lost and unloved,
Christ who gave the keys of the kingdom to his followers,
Christ who opened the door from death to resurrection,
bless us and keep us in the knowledge of hope, grace and love. Amen

Take a short time of reflection, with music (perhaps The Lark Ascending *by Ralph Vaughan Williams). Finish with refreshments.*

Reflections for the worship leader

A biblical reflection

Perhaps the first reading that comes to mind for the theme of 'keys to the door' is about Jesus giving the keys of the kingdom of heaven to Peter (Matthew 16:13–20), although this passage, has been (and, in places, remains) the root of disagreements between and within Christian traditions, including on the issue of women's ordination.

In biblical times, keys were a symbol of authority. The Gospels tell us that Jesus warned the scribes and Pharisees about their hypocrisy in the way they held the keys to knowledge and locked people out of the kingdom of heaven (Matthew 23:13; Luke 11:52). In the Bible reading for this service, we hear that the keys of the kingdom of heaven clearly belong to Jesus, the Christ, and Peter received them because he recognised Jesus as the Messiah. He was given the responsibility, through his ministry, of unlocking the way of Christ to others. It was a special moment, but did it mean that Peter had become the ultimate 'super disciple'? The very next verses remind us of one of Peter's misjudgements: Jesus said, 'Get behind me, Satan' (Matthew 16:23) when Peter declared that Jesus could not suffer and die. His mind was still locked into the worldly sphere, not the divine. At that moment, could Jesus have said, 'I want the keys back'?

Peter's discipleship was full of special moments of clarity, misunderstanding, denial and forgiveness. He was entrusted to open the doors of the gospel for many people, and his work was both vital and successful. But the same is true of many other followers of Jesus. We know little of Joanna, Thaddaeus, Susanna and others who found fullness of life after encountering Jesus, but they too were given keys to open doors of faith for others.

A spiritual reflection: 'Keys'

Jangling, essential
keys unlocking doors to the
safety of routine.

Silent, forgotten
keys waiting to unlock the
garden of Eden.

Windows

Arrange a focus table with a candle and cross, a bucket, chamois leather, a cloth designed for window cleaning and a photograph or card of a stained-glass window from the local church or cathedral (if appropriate, have one for each person within the group for prayer time).

Welcome and introduction

Today we shall think about windows, from cleaning them to the many views they have given us of life and faith.

Opening prayers

Introduce the response, 'God is with us: God is with us.'

We gather to look towards the presence of God
our Creator.
God is with us: **God is with us.**

We gather to look towards God, made known in Christ
our Saviour.
God is with us: **God is with us.**

We gather to look towards God who is made known
through the Holy Spirit.
God is with us: **God is with us.**

We say together the Lord's Prayer.

Conversation starters

- There are all kinds of special cloths designed to be the answer to cleaning windows, but can you beat old-fashioned window leather?
- Did you like cleaning windows or did you leave them as long as possible? What was your secret ingredient for cleaning windows? Do you have any stories about window cleaners?
- Do you remember the views from your childhood home? Do you have memories of the blackout and windows that were 'blown out' during the war?
- Did you get into trouble for looking out of the window during lessons at school?
- Do you remember any views from workplace windows?
- Did you have a favourite shop window when you were young? Were window displays changed on a regular basis by shop owners? Do you have any memories of seasonal displays in local shops?
- Have you ever found something interesting or amusing in an advert in a shop window?
- If you moved house, did you miss a particular view or gain a more interesting one? Is there a favourite view that you still cherish?
- What do you think about double glazing and triple glazing?
- New expressions have developed that use 'windows' as an image or metaphor, such as 'window in the weather', or 'transfer window' from the world of football. Can you think of any more?
- Does anyone use the 'Windows' computer operating system?

- What do you think about the stained-glass windows in your church?
- Do you have a favourite stained-glass window in a church or cathedral?
- How do stained-glass windows connect us to our faith?

Hymn suggestions

- Dear Lord and Father of mankind
- Praise to the holiest in the height

Bible reading and introduction

Today's reading is an extract from the book of Daniel, reminding us of the time when the people of Israel were in exile in Babylon. Daniel had a privileged position in the king's court but was envied by some of the Babylonian officials, who plotted to be rid of him. In this story we see the strength of Daniel's faith as he refuses to compromise his faith. He kneels to pray, looking through the windows of his home, looking towards the home of his faith, looking to God.

> So the presidents and satraps conspired and came to the king and said to him, 'O King Darius, live for ever! All the presidents of the kingdom, the prefects and the satraps, the counsellors and the governors, are agreed that the king should establish an ordinance and enforce an interdict, that whoever prays to anyone, divine or human, for thirty days, except to you, O king, shall be thrown into a den of lions. Now, O king, establish the interdict and sign the document, so that it cannot be changed, according to the law of

the Medes and the Persians, which cannot be revoked.'
Therefore King Darius signed the document and interdict.

Although Daniel knew that the document had been signed, he continued to go to his house, which had windows in its upper room open towards Jerusalem, and to get down on his knees three times a day to pray to his God and praise him, just as he had done previously.

DANIEL 6:6–10

Prayers

Ask for prayer requests. Introduce the prayer response, 'God of eternity: hear our prayer'.

We look through the windows of our worship
place to the view beyond and give thanks for
....
God of eternity: **hear our prayer.**

We think of the stained-glass windows that we
have admired in churches and cathedrals, and give
thanks for the details that connect us to the gospel
.... *(Add an appropriate prayer, from conversation shared or using the postcard or picture on the focus table. For example, 'Here at St Peters, we give thanks for the details that connect us to the gospel: the crucified and risen Jesus with staff in hand as shepherd of all his sheep, bread and fish reminding us of the feeding of the 5000, the last supper and resurrection meals, Peter being commissioned to tend and feed Jesus' sheep.)*
God of eternity: **hear our prayer.**

We pray that we may be faithful in prayer and worship, holding the example of Daniel in our minds and hearts. In faith we bring before God all those who need our prayer. For those whose view is darkened by war or disaster:
God of eternity: **hear our prayer.**

For those whose horizons are limited by illness and anxiety:
God of eternity: **hear our prayer.**

For those who have seen the curtain of life close and mourn the loss of loved ones:
God of eternity: **hear our prayer.**

And as we look to a view of heaven, we remember that Jesus said, 'Do not let your hearts be troubled. Believe in God, believe also in me. In my Father's house there are many dwelling places' (John 14:1–2).

We give thanks that Jesus is the Alpha and Omega, the beginning and the end. Thanks be to God. Amen

Closing hymn suggestions

- Be thou my vision
- May the mind of Christ my Saviour

A blessing

As Daniel knelt before his window, so we look to God's blessing made known in Christ.

> Be thou my vision, O Lord of my heart,
> Be all else but naught to me, save that thou art;
> Thou my best thought in the day and the night,
> Both waking and sleeping, thy presence my light.[10]

> May the blessing of God's love and grace rest upon us
> and remain with us always. Amen

Finish with refreshments.

Reflections for the worship leader

A biblical reflection

A dear friend once gave me a 'view through a window' of what it means to be in exile. It was during the time when I had the privilege of working in an urban parish. She was one of the first people I encountered there and initially she appeared reluctant to communicate beyond the niceties of Sunday encounters. After a few weeks, though, she thrust a video into my hand and, when I viewed the contents, I realised that I had had absolutely no comprehension of her story.[11]

My friend's home had disappeared in the eruption of the Soufrière Hills volcano, Montserrat, in the mid-1990s; she had lost everything. Eventually she had made her way to Britain, where she, her unborn child and her daughter found a place of safety. Along with many other refugees, she was in exile but determined to make a new home and a new life for her family. The views she had loved were gone; the worshipping community that had been at the heart of her life was scattered, but, with steadfast trust in God, her window of faith remained clear and bright and she found new beginnings.

Our reading today is from the book of Daniel, written in the context of the Jewish exile. It is a book of stories and dream visions built around the figure of Daniel, a faithful Jew in exile from the defeated city of Jerusalem. Daniel is portrayed as a wise counsellor to the kings of Babylon, successfully interpreting their visions, but envied by Babylonian officials. All kinds of traps were set to remove him from his office, but, each time, God intervened, saving him from death. One of the most famous and best-loved stories, 'Daniel in the lions' den', describes a time when an edict was issued, proclaiming that a person found praying to any being, divine or human, other than the king, would be thrown to the lions. Daniel would not compromise his faith, and prayer was an essential part of his life, so three times a day he praised God and asked for God's mercy.

His prayer took place in an upper room with windows open towards Jerusalem, his spiritual home. The windows are but a tiny detail within the story, yet they speak powerfully of looking to God, being faithful to God and trusting in God.

A spiritual reflection

See windows open in scripture
to breathtaking escapes,
freedom
and fullness of life.

The prostitute Rahab,
deceiving her own people,
shielding invaders and
offering her people's enemy
a window of escape (Joshua 2:15).

Saul, filled with a spirit of envy,
plotted David's death,
and had his men 'staked out'
to track his rival's movements;
but Michal,
daughter of Saul and wife of David,
opened a window to freedom (1 Samuel 19:12).

Paul, persecuted and pursued,
found himself cornered in Damascus,
but friends in Christ
opened a window,
releasing Paul
and releasing
the word of Christ (2 Corinthians 11:33).

So many possible windows of escape for the Christ—
to opt out of Calvary,
to let Lazarus lie,
to leave the tables in the temple,
to let the Pharisees be,
to walk away as disciples slept in Gethsemane.
But instead, our window to life—
fullness of life,
eternal life—
is flung wide open
in the frame of Christ's cross.

Curtains

Arrange a focus table with the cross and candle, plus some sample curtain fabric and a spare curtain—perhaps one that you have been keeping in case it might be useful.

Welcome and introduction

Curtains are the theme for our service today. *(If applicable, draw attention to curtains or blinds—or the absence of them—in the worship area. Perhaps there is a draught-excluding curtain over a door.)*

Curtains or blinds are an essential household item, helping to keep the cold or sunlight out and giving privacy. We begin by sharing our thoughts about curtains in the home and beyond, and will look at curtains in biblical times later in the service.

Conversation starters

- Do you prefer curtains or blinds, or a combination of the two?
- Who has bought ready-made curtains and who has made their own?
- If you made curtains, where did you buy the fabric—local shops, the market or fabric warehouses? Where have you found a good bargain?

- Curtain making is quite an art, especially if they have loose linings or fitted ones, but sometimes the most difficult job can be finding somewhere to cut them out. Where would you go to cut out curtains for a French window?
- Did you have different curtains for summer and winter? Do you always draw the curtains in the evening?
- Do you have memories of curtains at the cinema? Where have you seen some splendid theatre curtains? If you watched the Morecambe and Wise show, do you remember how Eric and Ernie used the curtain?
- Hospitals often had large open wards, but today the wards tend to be smaller, with curtains to go round each bed. Do you think the curtains give enough privacy?
- The tradition of closing the house curtains on the day of a funeral was once widespread, but is it as common now?
- There are different reactions to the closing of curtains during the prayer of committal at a crematorium. Some people like them to be closed, while others prefer them to remain open. How do you feel about this?

Our Bible reading today will be about the curtain that was torn in two at the time of the crucifixion.

Hymn suggestions

- O God, our help in ages past
- Praise to the holiest in the height

Take other suggestions from the group.

Opening prayers

Introduce the responses, 'Lord, have mercy' and 'Christ, have mercy', to be said towards the end of this prayer.

We come before God with thanks for the many details of our lives and homes that are precious to us now. We give thanks, too, that your Son, our Saviour Jesus Christ, lived in an ordinary home and understands the thoughts of our hearts.

We are mindful that we are not always the people God wills us to be, and so we bring to our forgiving Lord those times when we have seemed to draw the curtains, to avoid people and situations that were not convenient.

We bring to our forgiving Lord the times when fear has blinded us to the needs of others.

We bring to our forgiving Lord the times when we have not opened our hearts and minds to go the extra mile.

Lord, have mercy: **Lord, have mercy.**
Christ, have mercy: **Christ, have mercy.**
Lord, have mercy: **Lord, have mercy.**

May Almighty God draw back the curtain of our inadequacies to reveal his forgiving love. Amen

Bible reading and introduction

There are not many references to curtains in the Bible, but there are some in the Old Testament, giving precise details of the curtains to be made for the tabernacle, the portable dwelling-place for the presence of God. There is a wonderful description in the book of Exodus: 'Moreover you shall make the tabernacle with ten curtains of fine twisted linen, and blue, purple and crimson yarns; you shall make them with a cherubim skilfully worked into them' (26:1), and this is followed by many more details. The temple in Jerusalem was built to supersede the tabernacle, but it is interesting that the same colour and style of curtain was created by Solomon for the Holy of Holies, the most sacred part of the temple (2 Chronicles 3:14).

Solomon's temple was destroyed by the Babylonians but was rebuilt after the Jewish people returned from exile, and a further rebuilding and refurbishment was begun in 19BC by Herod the Great. The Holy of Holies continued to be curtained off, with only the high priest being allowed into this sacred space, and only on the Day of Atonement. In the account of Jesus' crucifixion, we hear more about the curtain in the temple.

> It was now about noon, and darkness came over the whole land until three in the afternoon, while the sun's light failed; and the curtain of the temple was torn in two. Then Jesus, crying with a loud voice, said, 'Father, into your hands I commend my spirit.' Having said this, he breathed his last. When the centurion saw what had taken place, he praised God and said, 'Certainly this man was innocent.' And when all the crowds who had gathered there for this spectacle saw what had taken place, they returned home, beating their breasts.
>
> LUKE 23:44–48

The tearing of the curtain is a powerful image to express that God had been made visible in Christ, present for all people, even a Roman centurion.

Prayers

Introduce the prayer response 'Lord, in your mercy: hear our prayer'.

We have a few moments of silence to bring to God the times in our lives when we felt as if a curtain had been opened and we saw and understood life with great clarity.
Lord, in your mercy: **hear our prayer.**

We remember times when curtains were drawn and we became aware of the significance of the closing of a life and the respect that was thus expressed. We remember friends, neighbours and family for whom we closed curtains. We name them aloud or in the silence of our hearts.
Lord, in your mercy: **hear our prayer.**

We remember the faithfulness of those who carried the tabernacle in the wilderness and those who worshipped in the temple in Jerusalem, for their story was part of Jesus' faith and is part of ours. We give thanks that Jesus was prepared to sacrifice his life, that all may clearly see the love of God.
Lord, in your mercy: **hear our prayer.**

We say together the Lord's Prayer.

Closing hymn suggestions

- Jesus shall reign
- Meekness and majesty

Blessing

God of our daily lives,
as we return to our homes
bless us with the peace of your presence,
the warmth of your love
and the hope of eternal life.
In the name of the Father and the Son
and the Holy Spirit. Amen

Finish with refreshments.

Reflections for the worship leader

A biblical reflection

Have you not known? Have you not heard?
Has it not been told you from the beginning?
Have you not understood from the foundations of the earth?
It is he who sits above the circle of the earth,
and its inhabitants are like grasshoppers;
who stretches out the heavens like a curtain,
and spreads them like a tent to live in;
who brings princes to naught,
and makes the rulers of the earth as nothing.
ISAIAH 40:21–23

I wonder who read Isaiah's words, or remembered them and breathed life into them as they were imparted with wonder, love and hope. I imagine the nation in exile, wondering if they would ever return to their homeland, if the temple could be rebuilt and if it all really mattered. Then someone strong in faith would bring the prophet's words to life, and those listening would hear the assurance that God is Creator and Lord of all time, far more powerful than princes and rulers. He is the one true God, concerned for the weakest and always with those who hope in the Lord. What a wonderful image to walk with—being wrapped in the curtain of all that God has created, the fabric of creation, as well as all that is beyond the horizon, the ultimate tent of hospitality, protection and care.

This is an image of God's presence far removed from what institutional religion had created. The temple, with its hierarchical leadership, was understood as being crucial to the relationship between God and humanity; it was a place of limited access for Gentiles and women, a place of compulsory and often expensive rituals, and yet there were the faithful people who prayed in steadfast love of God, those who taught with wisdom, and those in Jesus' time who watched and waited for the promised one (Luke 2:25, 36; 23:50–51). At the heart of the temple, the Holy of Holies was veiled by a curtain. I wonder if it was the same fabric and colour as the one that hung in the tabernacle or in Solomon's temple (2 Chronicles 3:14). I wonder if a cherubim was woven into it.

The curtain screened the sacred place that no one except the high priest could see or enter. God had been securely wrapped up by the institution, so all was well with heaven and earth. Then, one day, a troublesome rabbi was crucified, the curtain tore and it was clear for all, even a Roman centurion, to see that the power of heaven itself had been released.

A spiritual reflection

The following reflection describes a Good Friday family service at St Peter's Church, Hall Green, Birmingham.

It was Good Friday,
10.00 am, the time for family service.
A cross dominated the worship space.

Prayers prepared, dance and drama rehearsed,
instruments tuned, readings practised.
What seemed like the largest piece of fabric ever
had been purchased
and carefully draped over portable rails,
placed so that the altar was screened from view,
the way to the sanctuary blocked.

The church did not look right.

In Maundy Thursday tradition,
the church had been stripped
of fabric and furniture,
of candles and cassocks—
but what was this giant curtain doing?
This was Good Friday:
shouldn't the altar be visible?

Words and music told the story
of Jesus taking, blessing, breaking and sharing bread
and, in the same way, taking the cup of wine,
saying, 'Do this and remember me.
This is my body broken for you;
this is my blood shed for you.'
Mime depicted prayer in the garden;
stamping feet told of soldiers, betrayal and arrest;

arms outstretched, heads bowed to represent
crucifixion.

Then suddenly, without warning,
the rails were pulled apart,
the fabric ripped;
the sound of tearing filled the church.
Silence fell,
absolute silence.
The altar was restored to our sight,
its details noticeable after absence—
shaped by a carpenter's hands,
the patterns of a tree of life visible.
The simplicity of its design
gave it a sense of belonging—
a connection not just to ritual but to gathering,
as Jesus gathered with his disciples at table.

We gathered around it.
Some needed to steady themselves against it;
little ones crept under it;
hands reached out to touch.
We prayed for the world and one another,
for the gift of Christ's life and death.

Behind were the dazzling colours
of a resurrection window,
yet in this moment it was not seen.
You see, some had never stood in this place before,
and now they saw a different view.
Now was the time to pause and wait
before looking beyond to the brightness
of resurrection Sunday.

Light

Arrange a focus table with a cross and a large candle surrounded by a circle of four smaller candles. Provide a lighter and snuffer to be used during the prayers.

Welcome and introduction

We often take light for granted but, when the nights draw in, we realise how much we miss it. We are familiar with light as an image of God, but today we shall consider the problems with that image for those who are blind and live in darkness.

Opening prayers

Introduce the prayer response, 'We praise you: we praise you' and the repetition of 'Lord, have mercy' and 'Christ, have mercy'.

God, at work in the light and darkness of creation
We praise you; **we praise you.**

Christ, the light and life of all people
We praise you; **we praise you.**

Holy Spirit, the guiding light
We praise you; **we praise you.**

We think of the times when we have separated ourselves from God's love, when we have not found time for others, when our words have hurt them, when we have not reflected the light of God's love.

We spend a few moments in silence.

Lord, have mercy: **Lord have mercy.**
Christ, have mercy: **Christ, have mercy.**
Lord, have mercy: **Lord, have mercy.**

May God forgive us, may Christ renew us and may the Holy Spirit be our guide. Amen

Read aloud a denominational prayer or one that is familiar to the group, or simply use the following.

Gracious God, we pray that the light of your love will shine in our hearts as we worship you today. Amen

Conversation starters

- With a flick of a switch, the light comes on. Do we take it for granted? Do you have memories of gas light?
- When you were younger, what was the rule about turning lights off or leaving them on? Who shouted, 'Turn them off'?
- There is the possibility of power cuts when weather conditions are difficult. What kind of precautions do you take?
- The light changes according to the seasons. How do you feel in autumn and winter? Do you look forward to the shortest day, knowing that the days will begin to draw

out? Do you see all the dust around the house when the days lengthen?

- It is amazing how, even in our own country, the hours of daylight differ greatly between north and south. Has anyone lived in both northern and southern parts of the country? Did you notice a difference in the light?
- Has anyone travelled to different parts of the world and experienced much shorter or longer days, or seen the sun disappearing so quickly that there was hardly any evening time?
- Is the darkness a friend or foe?
- Do you enjoy candlelight in church? Are there any services that stand out in your mind, at which candles have been used?

If you have a copy, introduce John Hull's book, Touching the Rock, *which speaks of living in total blindness. Choose some paragraphs to read that reveal the problems of using the image of light for God, for people who are blind.*[12]

Hymn suggestions

- Christ, be our light
- Immortal, invisible
- Jesus shall reign

Take other suggestions from the group.

Bible reading and introduction

The first verses from the Gospel of John are some of the best-known and best-loved verses in the Bible. They give us a picture of Christ as the Word, Christ as life, and his life as a light for all people—a light that shines in any time and any circumstance.

In the beginning was the Word, and the Word was with God, and the Word was God. He was in the beginning with God. All things came into being through him, and without him not one thing came into being. What has come into being in him was life, and the life was the light of all people. The light shines in the darkness, and the darkness did not overcome it.

There was a man sent from God, whose name was John. He came as a witness to testify to the light, so that all might believe through him. He himself was not the light, but he came to testify to the light. The true light, which enlightens everyone, was coming into the world.

JOHN 1:1–9

Prayers

You will need to use a large candle, surrounded by a circle of four small candles, on the focus table. Introduce the prayer response, 'Christ, our light: hear our prayer.'

We light the large candle in the centre to remind us of the steadfast love of God, known in Christ and present in the power of the Holy Spirit.

We light a candle for ourselves, to remind us of the brightness and warmth of God's love for us.

In a few moments of silence, let us give thanks for Christ in our life.

Christ, our light: **hear our prayer.**

We light the second candle for this group, for all who plan and organise it, all who attend and for groups we have belonged to throughout our lives.

In a few moments resting in God's presence, we name aloud or in silence the people who have shared our journey in life.
Christ, our light: **hear our prayer.**

We light the third candle for those with whom we have connections but whom we do not see very often, remembering members of our families and friends.

In a few moments of silence, we name in God's presence those from whom we are separated.
Christ, our light: **hear our prayer.**

We light the fourth candle for those we have loved and lost, those whose souls rest in the kingdom of heaven.

In a few moments of silence, we name in God's presence those who have died.
Christ, our light: **hear our prayer.**

As seasons come and go, as light fades and returns, we give thanks for the life-light of God's love made known to us in Christ, a love that has not faded or slipped away but remains in our hearts. Amen

We say together the Lord's Prayer.

Take time for reflection while quiet music plays—for example, a Taizé chant such as 'The Lord is my light', or the anthem 'Hail, gladdening light'.

Extinguish the candles while reading these verses from Psalm 139:11–12:

If I say, 'Surely the darkness shall cover me, and the light around me become night', even the darkness is not dark to you; the night is as bright as the day, for darkness is as light to you.

As the candlelight is snuffed out, we remember that, just as the smoke rises and mingles with us, so too does the love of God.

A blessing

The Lord make his face to shine upon you, and be gracious to you; the Lord lift up his countenance upon you, and give you peace. Amen (Numbers 6:25–26)

Finish with refreshments.

Reflections for the worship leader

A biblical reflection

Biblical images of light are plentiful, including sunlight, moonlight and starlight in creation (Genesis 1:16), the prophetic movement from darkness and despair to light and hope (for example, Isaiah 9:2), and psalms praising God as our light and salvation (for example, Psalm 27:1).

At the same time, there are other issues to bear in mind. Professor John Hull's book, *Touching the Rock*, tells of the reality and personal significance of being totally blind. Professor Hull reminds us that, for a person in deep blindness, to represent light as goodness and darkness as evil is problematic. He tells how he, as a person living in total darkness, has had times of frustration, particularly when liturgy filled with images of light becomes exclusive and insensitive.[13] There is solace to be found, however, particularly from a psalmist:

> *If I say, 'Surely the darkness shall cover me, and the light around me become night', even the darkness is not dark to you; the night is as bright as the day, for darkness is as light to you (Psalm 139:11–12).*

Light remains a powerful image, not least in the prologue to John's Gospel, where we read, 'The light shines in the darkness, and the darkness did not overcome it' (1:4). It is well worth reading John 1 in a selection of Bible translations, should the familiarity of these words lose their impact. *The Message*, for example, says, 'The Life-Light blazed out of the darkness; the darkness couldn't put it out.'

While thinking about light, I was reminded of a priest speaking at a Christmas celebration service where preschool children, all under four years of age, were holding glow candles (a non-toxic version of glow sticks). He asked them to hide the glow candles under their costumes and then bring them out again. He spoke of how we experience times when we see or know that the Christ-light is present and times when we feel that it is hidden, but know that it is there, nevertheless.

A spiritual reflection: the light in Advent darkness

As the light fades
and November days slip into December,
Advent is upon us.
Christmas decorations, trees and garlands
light up our streets,
Advent evenings wrap around our lives,

the dark no longer just for sleeping hours
but our companion as we go about our daily tasks.

And still the hours of light decrease,
yet on those rare days when the sky is clear,
and in that brief time after dawn and just before dusk,
there is a clarity of light
unlike at any other time of year—
breathtaking transparency in town or country,
moments to bring to mind the creative love of God
and the power of God's love
in the coming of the Christmas gift,
the Christ-light.

Chairs

Arrange the worship space to include an empty chair with a 'special' cushion and a throw over it.

Welcome and introduction

Our theme today is 'chairs'. We shall spend some time imagining that Jesus is sitting in this empty chair and what we might say to him.

Conversation starters

- 'Are you sitting comfortably? Then I'll begin.' Who said it and when? *(BBC radio* Listen with Mother *at 1.45 pm, just before* Woman's Hour.*)*
- Do you remember 'Halfway down the stairs is a stair where I sit' from the poem by A.A. Milne? *(Have a copy to read, if appropriate.)*
- Some chairs are comfortable and others are not so comfort able. How do they rate here?
- When you were young, who sat on the best chairs? Were pets allowed on chairs?
- Do you say 'antimacassars' or 'chair back and arm covers'?
- Garden chairs and furniture are very popular now. Was it the same when you were younger?

- When you went to the beach, did you have collapsible deckchairs? Could you put them up in one go?
- Do you remember anyone you sat next to at school? How did teachers arrange classrooms—according to pupils' ability or in alphabetical order of their names?
- If you visited the theatre or cinema, did you usually have the best seats in the house or were you up 'in the gods'? Perhaps we shouldn't ask about the back row of the cinema!
- Are people willing to find a chair or give up a chair for those who are frail?
- Do you remember Rosa Parks' story?
- Have you ever had to use a wheelchair? What do you think about mobility scooters?
- Do/did you always sit in the same place in church? How do you feel about pews or chairs in church?
- Look to the empty chair and to imagine Jesus sitting there. What would you say to him?

Opening prayers

Create a prayer that gathers together some of the ideas that have emerged from conversation, or use the following words.

As we have gathered in the presence of God, made known in Jesus Christ and the Holy Spirit, we bring with us our thoughts, our concerns and our hopes. We give thanks that Jesus came to serve, sat with people from many different backgrounds and was willing to take the cup of suffering and give his life in love. Amen

Say together the adaptation of Thomas Ken's prayer (see page 21) or read another appropriate prayer aloud.

Suggested hymns

- Angel voices ever singing
- At the name of Jesus

Take other suggestions from the group.

Bible reading and introduction

Our reading from Mark's Gospel speaks of the disciples wanting the best seats in the kingdom of heaven. Jesus had to explain to them what it would really mean to be seated with him.

James and John, the sons of Zebedee, came forward to him and said to him, 'Teacher, we want you to do for us whatever we ask of you.' And he said to them, 'What is it you want me to do for you?' And they said to him, 'Grant us to sit, one at your right hand and one at your left, in your glory.' But Jesus said to them, 'You do not know what you are asking. Are you able to drink the cup that I drink, or be baptised with the baptism that I am baptised with?' They replied, 'We are able.' Then Jesus said to them, 'The cup that I drink you will drink; and with the baptism with which I am baptised, you will be baptised; but to sit at my right hand or at my left is not mine to grant, but it is for those for whom it has been prepared.'

When the ten heard this, they began to be angry with James and John. So Jesus called them and said to them, 'You know that among the Gentiles those whom they recognise as their rulers lord it over them, and their great ones are tyrants over them. But it is not so among you; but whoever

wishes to become great among you must be your servant, and whoever wishes to be first among you must be slave of all. For the Son of Man came not to be served but to serve, and to give his life a ransom for many.'
MARK 10:35–45

Prayers

Introduce the prayer response, 'Lord, hear us: Lord, graciously hear us.' Explain that there will be a short pause at the end of each section of prayer, for personal silent prayers.

We give thanks to God for Jesus, who got up from where he was sitting to wash his disciples' feet, and asked that they would do the same.
Lord, hear us: **Lord, graciously hear us.**

We give thanks for the disciples, who left their comfortable seats to follow Jesus and, when life was difficult after his death and resurrection, did not choose to take a back seat.
Lord, hear us: **Lord, graciously hear us.**

We think of those who sit in positions of power and authority, and we pray that they may be blessed with wisdom and discernment.
Lord, hear us: **Lord, graciously hear us.**

We remember the people who have sat next to us at home, at work and in our group, and we give thanks for their company.
Lord, hear us: **Lord, graciously hear us.**

We remember those moments when we have sunk into a chair at the end of a long day, and we give thanks for the busy days of our lives.
Lord, hear us: **Lord, graciously hear us.**

We remember times when friends and family have needed us to assist them with a chair, and we give thanks that, in that simple act, we learnt about serving as you served us.
Lord, hear us: **Lord, graciously hear us.**

We remember that, one day, we too may need assistance, and we pray that others will meet our needs with kindness.
Lord, hear us: **Lord, graciously hear us.**

We recall words from the book of Revelation: 'And the one who was seated on the throne said, "See, I am making all things new." Also he said, "Write this, for these words are trustworthy and true." Then he said to me, "It is done! I am the Alpha and the Omega, the beginning and the end. To the thirsty I will give water as a gift from the spring of the water of life"' (Revelation 21:5–6).

We give thanks, Lord, that you sit beside us to renew and refresh our faith. In you we trust. Amen

Say the Lord's Prayer together.

Take time for reflection while quiet music plays (for example, Pachelbel's Canon *or* Gymnopédie *by Erik Satie.*

A blessing

May the love of God enfold us and the blessing of God Almighty, the Father, the Son and the Holy Spirit, be among us, and remain with us always. Amen
COMMON WORSHIP

Finish with refreshments.

Reflections for the worship leader

A biblical reflection

There is a wonderful description, in Exodus 25:17–22, of God directing Moses to make a 'mercy seat' of pure gold. God said, 'From above the mercy seat, from between the two cherubim that are on the ark of the covenant, I will deliver to you all my commands for the Israelites' (v. 22). The tabernacle containing the ark of the covenant, with its mercy seat, became 'holy ground' symbolising the relationship and presence of God with the people of Israel and the authority of God in the nation's life.

The focus changed, however, when God's people demanded an earthly king (1 Samuel 8:6). Hannah, the mother of Samuel, sang that God 'lifts the needy from the ash heap, to make them sit with princes and inherit a seat of honour' (1 Samuel 2:8). This must have seemed an impossible vision throughout the era of the kings that followed. Many took their place on a throne, a seat of honour, and all too often they reflected earthly authority, power and glory, creating kingdoms far removed from the kingdom of God's love.

Yet Hannah's words echoed through the ages and, in the angel Gabriel's announcement to Mary that she will bear a son, we learn that 'the Lord God will give to him the throne of his ancestor David' (Luke 1:32). Kingship will be revealed and lived not from a throne in a palace, the seat of wealth and power, but in the vulnerability of a child who will sit in a peasant's home and later, in his ministry, will sit alongside the weak and rejected. Mary's song of praise, known as the Magnificat, is similar to Hannah's: with eloquent and subversive words, it speaks of God bringing down the powerful from their thrones (Luke 1:46–55).

Seats were the focus of controversy at times in Jesus' ministry: he spoke of the Pharisees loving to have the best seats in the synagogue (Luke 11:43), he overturned the seats of the dove sellers in the temple (Mark 11:15), and he confronted the disciples' self-centred requests for seats at his right and left hand in the kingdom of heaven (Matthew 20:20–23; Mark 10:35–40).

Mark and Matthew give differing perspectives regarding the seats of honour in eternal life. Mark has James and John boldly asking for a place at Jesus' side, and I personally like the detail of Mark's account. There is such honesty in the disciples' request—a sense that 'we want something out of this', similar to the way we all think at times, though we may not like to admit it. Their request is not affirmed, because Jesus declares that it is not his gift to grant. 'It is for those for whom it has been prepared' (v. 40), and will depend on faith and service to God.

The parallel passage in Matthew 20 has Salome, the mother of James and John, requesting seats at Jesus' right and left hand on behalf of her sons. Did Matthew perhaps think it would set a bad example for discipleship if he portrayed the followers asking for themselves? In any case, Jesus still does not grant the request, but in the previous chapter he promises thrones for all the disciples, as well as an inheritance for everyone who humbly serves God (Matthew 19:28–29).

We can understand that those who had literally sat next to Jesus during his earthly ministry might have had expectations about their future status. When we think that James, John and Peter were next to Jesus at some crucial moments—on the mount of transfiguration and at the raising of Jairus' daughter—then we can understand how they might have wanted the 'best seats in the house' in the future kingdom.

The account in Mark's Gospel is lively and candid. I wonder if the anger expressed by the other disciples (10:41) had a tone of self-righteousness. Would they never have made such a request for themselves or were they 'fed up to the back teeth' with hearing pleas for favouritism? Whatever the case, Jesus rapidly intervenes. He has explained the view from his seat three times before this moment: it is a view of painful suffering, death and resurrection. Even so, he tells them again that the glory and greatness they crave will come only through being a 'slave of all' (v. 44), living in total service to others. Can they sit comfortably in that 'seat'?

After Jesus' death and resurrection, the disciples would indeed discover that seat as they were persecuted and ostracised. Some, including James and Peter, faced cruel deaths ordered by those who sat on imperial thrones—King Herod of Agrippa, who ruled that James should be killed, and Emperor Nero, who had Peter crucified.

A spiritual reflection

Have you ever been caught out by chairs? I remember a Christmas morning in church when chairs had been rearranged so that the congregation could make a physical journey—sitting in one area for the Gathering, moving to the body of the church for the Liturgy of the Word, and gathering close to the altar for the Liturgy of the Sacrament. Many of the chairs were facing the entrance and font, allowing a wonderful view of latecomers expecting to sneak in unnoticed—not least one of my sons and his girlfriend. Their faces were a picture, and his brother and sister have never allowed the moment to be forgotten.

It was a new experience for me at theological college to see chairs in the chapel facing each other. There was no hiding behind anyone there. How would your local Sunday congregation react if everyone had to look at one another? In sacramental traditions, would the view of one another make the opening words of greeting and confession more meaningful, before turning to the lectern for the Gospel and gathering around the altar for Communion?

Where do our 'sages' sit in the life of the church? How can we make them more comfortable? What do they miss, and what do they love? When they are no longer able to sit in the body of the church, how do we physically and spiritually sit alongside them?

What does it say to us when we see chairs placed around the edge of a room in a care centre, facing a television that blares out unremitting daytime soaps and chat shows?

Zechariah, 'getting on in years' (Luke 1:7), sang a song of salvation with words that offer comfort to those who find ageing to be a time of sitting in darkness.

By the tender mercy of our God,
the dawn from on high will break upon us,
to give light to those who sit in darkness
and in the shadow of death,
to guide our feet into the way of peace. (Luke 1:78–79)

From fire to radiators

Arrange a focus table with a candle, a 'newspaper cracker' used for lighting a fire, and a large photograph of a fire within a home.

Welcome and introduction

There is nothing like an open fire to gather around—although it's perhaps not so good if you have to clear the ashes! Today we think about fires, heating and a meeting on a beach between Jesus and Peter.

Conversation starters

- What would we do without electric fires or central heating?
- Heating has changed enormously over the years. How do you feel about radiators: are they efficient but soulless?
- What was it like in your childhood days? Do you remember coal fires?
- Who was responsible for ordering coal? How was it delivered?
- Who had the job of lighting the fire? How and when did they do it? Who was responsible for clearing the ashes and how did you dispose of them?

- How often did the chimney sweep come? How did you prepare?
- Was washing dried around the fire?
- Did you cook anything on the fire—toast, potatoes or chestnuts?
- Do you remember the sound and smell of a fire? Did you look for pictures in the flames?
- Do you have stories of war-time fires caused by bombing?
- We see regular reports of forest fires in many different parts of the world, including our own; do you know anyone who has suffered because of them?
- Do you have any memories of campfires, bonfires and fireworks, or barbeques?
- Are there any fires that come to mind from Bible stories?

Opening prayers

Gracious God, kindle in us the fire of your love. As we meet to pray, may we know the warmth of God's love in our hearts and the glow of God's light in our minds. Amen

Read aloud a traditional prayer or one that is familiar to the group.

Hymn suggestions

- O thou who camest from above
- Colours of day
- Veni, Sancte Spiritus

Take other suggestions from the group.

Bible reading and introduction

In this resurrection reading you can almost feel the warmth of the charcoal fire on the shores of the Sea of Galilee and the warmth of Jesus' forgiving and embracing love as he speaks to his disciple, Peter.

> When they had gone ashore, they saw a charcoal fire there, with fish on it, and bread. Jesus said to them, 'Bring some of the fish that you have just caught.' So Simon Peter went aboard and hauled the net ashore, full of large fish, a hundred and fifty-three of them; and though there were so many, the net was not torn. Jesus said to them, 'Come and have breakfast.' Now none of the disciples dared to ask him, 'Who are you?' because they knew it was the Lord. Jesus came and took the bread and gave it to them, and did the same with the fish. This was now the third time that Jesus appeared to the disciples after he was raised from the dead.
>
> When they had finished breakfast, Jesus said to Simon Peter, 'Simon son of John, do you love me more than these?' He said to him, 'Yes, Lord; you know that I love you.' Jesus said to him, 'Feed my lambs.' A second time he said to him, 'Simon son of John, do you love me?' He said to him, 'Yes, Lord; you know that I love you.' Jesus said to him, 'Tend my sheep.' He said to him the third time, 'Simon son of John, do you love me?' Peter felt hurt because he said to him the third time, 'Do you love me?' And he said to him, 'Lord, you know everything; you know that I love you.' Jesus said to him, 'Feed my sheep.'
>
> JOHN 21:9–17

Prayers

Introduce the prayer response, 'Lord, in the warmth of your love: hear our prayer.'

As we remember fires and firelight, we think first of times and places where companionship around a fire has been difficult, where family has not been cosy or comfortable. We bring the ashes of discomfort and pain to our healing God.
Lord, in the warmth of your love: **hear our prayer.**

We think too of the times when we have failed to be the people you want us to be. We bring the ashes of our failure to our forgiving God.
Lord, in the warmth of your love: **hear our prayer.**

We give thanks that, in the disciple Peter, we see not denial, failure and guilt, but the way the love of Christ kindles a new beginning of forgiveness, hope and joy.
Lord, in the warmth of your love: **hear our prayer.**

We give thanks for the warmth of life, for all that is good, for people who have made a difference in our living. We spend a few moments in silence, bringing the flames of thanksgiving to our loving God.
Lord, in the warmth of your love: **hear our prayer.**

As we think of the gift of the years of our life, we bring our flames of concern and worry, the doubts that flicker in our minds, our questions about ageing and dying, and we pray that we may know your presence and peace with us.
Lord, in the warmth of your love: **hear our prayer.**

We thank you, Lord, for the fire of your love to light our journey. Lighten our darkness and brighten our days, that we may live as faithful followers.

We say together the Lord's Prayer.

A blessing

As we go from this place,
may the flame of God's eternal love go with us,
lighting the way in our daily lives;
and may the blessing of God
known as Father, Son and Holy Spirit,
surround and hold us until we meet again. Amen

Take time for reflection with some stirring music playing (for example, parts of Handel's Music for the Royal Fireworks*).*

Finish with refreshments.

Reflections for the worship leader

A biblical reflection

There are an enormous number of references to fire in the Bible, including the story of Moses and the bush that was ablaze but not consumed (Exodus 3:2–5), the story of Elijah on the mountain looking for God in the wind, earthquake and fire (1 Kings 19:11–12), the refiner's fire in Malachi 3:2–3, and John the Baptist's proclamation that the one to come 'will baptise you with the Holy Spirit and fire' (Matthew 3:11). Later, in the book of Acts, we read of the coming of the Holy Spirit upon the disciples, when 'divided tongues, as of fire, appeared among them, and a tongue rested on each of them' in the upper room (Acts 2:3).

How can the power and strength of the Holy Spirit be described? How can the fulfilment of Jesus' promise of an advocate, a helper (John 14:26), be put into words? The light and brightness, warmth and power of the mystery of resurrection life is captured in the image of resting flames, and we are left to wonder at the significance of this moment and how we ourselves might describe an experience of the Holy Spirit.

At the heart of two powerful New Testament stories are charcoal fires. Slaves and palace officials had made a charcoal fire in the courtyard of the high priest when Jesus was arrested. Peter ventured there and, as the coals glowed, he denied his discipleship (John 18:15–27). He broke down, weeping bitterly. In the first minutes of a fear-filled dawn, the embers grew cold and Peter disappeared from sight.

Another fire was lit just after daybreak as the fishermen disciples were attempting to find normality, after the resurrection. They had failed to get a catch, but then, with Christ directing them, as had happened once before, their fishing nets were filled. As Peter recognised the risen Lord, he was drawn again to a charcoal fire (John 21:1–9).

A spiritual reflection: Fire

Fire is so distant now.
Radiators, heaters, under-floor heating
have taken the reality of fire from our lives.
Bonfires forbidden by smokeless zones,
campfires in designated areas only,
the flames of Bonfire Night distanced
by health and safety,
not even stubble-burning except with permission.

Only a chimney wisp of smoke from country cottages
or an occasional open fire
remind us of the smell,
the dancing, crackling red-orange light of fire.

But there are other, terrible, images of fire.
History sends a reminder of the chimneys of Auschwitz,
television brings reminders of pyres of burning animals,
victims of foot and mouth.
When news breaks of destructive wildfires
in far-off places,
pictures appear and, within a day or so, disappear.

Old Testament stories speak of God's people
conquering with fire.
Jericho's walls fell and the city was burned,
while Elijah almost played with the power of God
'If I am a man of God, let fire come down from heaven
and consume you and your fifty.
Then fire came down from heaven' (2 Kings 1:10).

Fire so often brings death and destruction.
Perhaps it is better that fire is so distant now.
But then the depth of the image of the love of God, that
burns 'with inextinguishable blaze',[14] is lost.
The bush lit with the passion of God;
the delivering love of a midwife-God, leading her
people 'in a pillar of fire by night' (Exodus 13:21);
the fragrant holiness of an encounter with God as
incense is placed on an altar fire (Leviticus 16:13).

Flames threaten to consume in New Testament times—
the fire of Roman rule
demanding that people gather

for their pagan emperor's census.
Yet God was not consumed
but transcended Roman commands
in the gift of a helpless child—
a child named by an angel
and nurtured by the warmth of Joseph and Mary's love.

This holy family fled for their lives,
to be warmed by sheltering fires
built in nooks and crannies
along the paths to Egypt,
and in these flames found a picture of God
kindling hope.

Imagine woodpiles, fires and flames
that cooked meals for Jesus—
flames at the home of Peter,
flames at the home of Zacchaeus,
flames at the home of Mary, Martha and Lazarus,
flames where the last supper was prepared.

When the embers lost their glow
and the fire of loyalty died,
the destructive fire of fear and hate led to the cross.
See the darkness that came over the whole land.
But, as darkness turned to dawning,
God's light blazed in the garden of resurrection;
forgiveness blazed by a charcoal fire;
love blazed in the gift of the Holy Spirit.

God of flame and fire,
kindle in us the fire of your love.

Tables

Arrange a focus table covered with a special tablecloth, a cross, and a place setting including mat, knife, fork, spoon, flowers and candle.

Welcome and introduction

We gather today, remembering the times we have sat at table with families and friends, with colleagues in the canteen or for times of fellowship over a cup of tea. We remember that Jesus, the Christ, sat at tables with friends and foes, and unexpected events often unfolded there.

Opening prayers

Read aloud some appropriate prayers from church liturgy, or use the following words.

We give thanks that Jesus sat at friends' tables to reveal the purposes of God's transforming love. Amen

Hymn suggestions

- Praise, my soul
- As we are gathered

Take other suggestions from the group.

Conversation starters

- Who set the table in your home? Did you have different tableware for everyday use and for high days and holidays?
- Whose company have you enjoyed around the table?
- What else was the table used for?
- Did your table have a story to tell in scratches, marks and burns?
- Who served meals or carved a Sunday roast? Who sat where?
- What do you think about table manners? What were the rules in your home?
- Did you (or do you) have a favourite table at a café?
- Do you have experience of tables at lunch clubs? How are they set?
- Do you have any experience of tables in hospitals or convalescent/rehabilitation centres?
- Vocabulary varies in churches: do you use the word altar or Communion table? What do you prefer and why?
- Did you sing or say a grace or a blessing of the table before meals?

Sing or say a grace known to the members of the group, and use it again before refreshments at the end of the service.

Thank you for the world so sweet,
thank you for the food we eat,
thank you for the birds that sing,
thank you, God, for everything.
EDITH RUTTER-LEATHAN

Bible reading and introduction

There is a lot going on around the table in our Bible reading, which is set at the home of Lazarus and his sisters. Mary is filled with love for Jesus, Judas is unable to see love at work, and the fragrance of love fills the house as Jesus is anointed.

> Six days before the Passover Jesus came to Bethany, the home of Lazarus, whom he had raised from the dead. There they gave a dinner for him. Martha served, and Lazarus was one of those at the table with him. Mary took a pound of costly perfume made of pure nard, anointed Jesus' feet, and wiped them with her hair. The house was filled with the fragrance of the perfume. But Judas Iscariot, one of his disciples (the one who was about to betray him), said, 'Why was this perfume not sold for three hundred denarii and the money given to the poor?' (He said this not because he cared about the poor, but because he was a thief; he kept the common purse and used to steal what was put into it.) Jesus said, 'Leave her alone. She bought it so that she might keep it for the day of my burial. You always have the poor with you, but you do not always have me.'
> JOHN 12:1–8

Prayers

Introduce the prayer response, 'God of grace: be with us.'

Gracious God, so often a table is at the heart of a home. We give thanks for the times we have sat with family and friends, learning, disagreeing, sharing and laughing.
God of grace: **be with us.**

We think too of the empty places at our table, as people we have loved have departed this life. We give thanks for the memories we treasure.
God of grace: **be with us.**

We pray for grace, that wherever we may find ourselves in coming years, in hospitals, residential homes or limited to a single room, we may take our place at table in the knowledge that Christ is alongside us.
God of grace: **be with us.**

We give thanks for the altars and Communion tables that we have gathered around in churches and halls throughout our lives. We give thanks for those who make intricate altar cloths, those who prepare and serve at the table and those who take, bless and break bread. At your table, Lord, we remember all that has been given for us.
God of grace: **be with us.**

As we remember Jesus gathering with the rich and poor, the sick and unloved, we give thanks for the love he shared. Our television screens bring us images of people without shelter, without adequate food or a place to eat with dignity, and so we pray for the work of aid agencies, charities and international relief workers. In particular we remember the people of *[add place names, as appropriate]*.
God of grace: **be with us.**

Say together the Lord's Prayer and the adaptation of Thomas Ken's prayer *(see page 21)**.*

Closing hymn suggestions

- Lord, for the years
- The King of Love

A blessing

Invite the group to repeat the word 'Amen' after each sentence of this blessing.

> As we look to our table of refreshments, tea and biscuits to cheer us on our way, so we pray that God will bless us with grace. Amen. **Amen**
> The love of Christ will be in our fellowship.
> Amen. **Amen**
> The Holy Spirit will journey with us. Amen. **Amen**

Finish with refreshments preceded by a grace.

Reflections for the worship leader

A biblical reflection

There are descriptions of magnificent ceremonial tables and altars in the Old Testament. The book of Exodus gives precise measurements for the table for the 'bread of the Presence', a part of the furnishings of the portable tabernacle. It was made of acacia wood and overlaid with gold (Exodus 25:23–24). Later, in the time of Solomon, a golden table for the bread of the Presence was made, for use in the Jerusalem temple (1 Kings 7:48).

Significant and wealthy people possessed tables, as we can see in the accounts of Saul, David and Solomon (1 Samuel 20:29; 2 Samuel 9:7; 1 Kings 4:27), but, even without a table, hospitality involving the sharing of food was most significant in relationships, encounters and response to strangers. Hospitable customs are seen in Abraham's encounter with the Lord at the oaks of Mamre (Genesis 18) and in the story of Ruth. In accordance with the social laws of the Jewish people, Ruth, though poverty-stricken and a stranger in Bethlehem, was allowed to glean in landowners' fields, and sat and ate with one named Boaz (Ruth 2).

In the New Testament, we don't find details of ceremonial furniture but we do hear of Jesus overturning the tables in the temple courtyards (Mark 11:15). We are constantly aware of Jesus being 'at table' with a wide variety of people, but again we assume that, in poorer homes, there would have just been a straw mat, whereas wealthier families would have had a table (see Jesus' encounter with the Syro-Phoenician woman in Mark 7:24–30 and at his friends' home in Bethany, in John 12:1–8). Of course, we think of Jesus at table with his followers for Passover the night before he died—the meal that we remember as the Last Supper. (We will think further about that meal during another service.) There is something about thinking of Jesus around a table with all kinds of people that brings us closer to him, allowing us to imagine him sitting with us, around our table.

One of the most beautiful 'table stories' is in John's Gospel, where, a few days before Passover, Jesus goes to the home of his dear friends Mary, Martha and Lazarus. As Jesus sits at their table, Mary anoints his feet, pouring out a pound of costly perfume (John 12:3). It is a moment filled with the depth of Mary's love and her understanding that Jesus will die. It is also a moment that displays Judas' total misunderstanding, and a moment when, in the fragrance of the perfume, the extravagance and cost of Jesus' love is tangible.

A spiritual reflection

Now, be honest:
to choose to sit in a comfy chair with
a meal on a tray at the end of a long day
is sometimes the easiest way,
despite risking gravy stains on your shirt!

Imagine homes where there is no table,
not even a tray,
where takeaways from a box, or chips in paper,
are the norm.

Consider people who yearn to sit at table
but, their bodies ageing and frail,
cannot take even a few steps.
Do they tire of trays and isolating tables
pushed up to beds and wheelchairs?

In towns and villages
where earthquake, tsunami, fire and war
have robbed homes of treasured tables,
how deep is the longing for a space, a place
where depleted families and lost friends
can gather again?

Where is a table
ready for company and conversation,
an open table for friend and stranger?
That table—solid wood, picnic blanket or even
upturned box—
has a value beyond Solomon's masterpiece,
for it is
a priceless connection to the Holy One.

Water

Arrange a focus table with a bottle of spring water, a jug of water and a glass.

Welcome and introduction

Our service today has the theme of water—something we so often take for granted. We shall think of flood waters, the waters of baptism and Jesus speaking of the living water.

Opening prayers

Read aloud the adapted prayer of Thomas Ken (see page 21) or another appropriate prayer.

A psalmist said, 'O God, you are my God, I seek you,
my soul thirsts for you' (Psalm 63:1). We pray that,
in fellowship and word, God may nourish our souls.
Amen

Conversation starters

- Do we take water for granted?
- Was hot water a luxury when you were young? Do you remember having just a cold tap or even a shared tap in the yard?

- Springs and wells were often a source of water; do you know of any local ones?
- What do you think about water meters?
- Do you buy bottled water? Do you drink it straight from the bottle?
- Have you noticed the effects of hard and soft water on appliances in different areas of the country?
- Over recent years, there have been many stories of flooding in Britain and across the world. Do you know anyone who has suffered in this way? What are the images from the media that stay with you? Have you ever lived somewhere that was prone to flooding?
- There are many charities that provide clean water and sanitation. Have you or your church ever supported one? *(Provide some information—for example, from WaterAid or the Busoga Trust.)*
- Have you ever been really thirsty?
- Water is a symbol often used in church services. Were you baptised or have you attended baptisms where there is a sprinkling of water or full immersion? What are your thoughts about this?
- Do you have a favourite 'watery' story from the Bible?

Hymn suggestions

- I heard the voice of Jesus say
- Jesus, lover of my soul
- Have you heard the raindrops?

Take other suggestions from the group.

Bible reading and introduction

John's Gospel tells of a meeting between Jesus and a Samaritan woman at a well. This was unusual because of the animosity between Jews and Samaritans. The conversation moved from a simple request for a drink to the offer of living water, the hope and love that only Jesus Christ can give.

> A Samaritan woman came to draw water, and Jesus said to her, 'Give me a drink.' (His disciples had gone to the city to buy food.) The Samaritan woman said to him, 'How is it that you, a Jew, ask a drink of me, a woman of Samaria?' (Jews do not share things in common with Samaritans.) Jesus answered her, 'If you knew the gift of God, and who it is that is saying to you, "Give me a drink", you would have asked him, and he would have given you living water.' The woman said to him, 'Sir, you have no bucket, and the well is deep. Where do you get that living water? Are you greater than our ancestor Jacob, who gave us the well, and with his sons and his flocks, drank from it?' Jesus said to her, 'Everyone who drinks of this water will be thirsty again, but those who drink of the water that I will give them will never be thirsty. The water that I will give will become in them a spring of water gushing up to eternal life.' The woman said to him, 'Sir, give me this water, so that I may never be thirsty or have to keep coming here to draw water.'
>
> JOHN 4:7–15

It began as an ordinary encounter and went on to reveal the life-giving nature of Jesus. In the following verses, as the woman speaks of the Messiah who is to come, Jesus affirms that he is the one.

Prayers

Ask for prayer requests. Introduce the prayer response, 'Lord in your mercy: hear our prayer.'

We give thanks that God has provided for our needs, giving us water to sustain and cleanse us.

We give thanks for scientists and engineers who have made it possible for us to have running water.

We think of the many beautiful reservoirs throughout our country, mindful that, in their construction, many people lost their homes and communities—their stories often forgotten.
Lord, in your mercy: **hear our prayer.**

There are many areas in the world that are affected by flooding. We hear the stories on the news and see the people's suffering, but we know little of what happens in the following months and years. We pray for all who live and work in those areas, that they may receive your compassion and strength to face the future. *[If necessary, compose an appropriate prayer for recent news of flooding or tsunamis.]*
Lord, in your mercy: **hear our prayer.**

As we think of Jesus going down into the waters of baptism and rising to be blessed by the Spirit of God, and later meeting a woman at a well where the gift of the living water was offered for all, so we spend a few moments reflecting on our baptism or those times when Jesus Christ has sustained us.

Take a short time for reflection while quiet music plays, evoking streams or the sea (for example, from the CD Sanctuary *by Celtic Waters.*[15] *This music could be played in the background for the closing prayers.*

We give thanks for Jesus, who gave us the living water of forgiveness, reconciliation and love to sustain our lives; and, through his death and resurrection, revealed the joy of eternal life. Amen

We say the Lord's Prayer together.

A blessing

Invite the group to repeat the 'Amen' at the end of each line of this blessing.

May God the Creator, who blessed the earth with
life-giving water, bless us. Amen. **Amen**
May Jesus the Christ, the water of life, bless us.
Amen. **Amen**
May the Holy Spirit, who was there in the beginning,
blessing creation, continue to bless us. Amen. **Amen**

Reflections for the worship leader

A biblical reflection

The sea, springs, streams and wells are significant throughout scripture, and water is used symbolically in church tradition, from sacramental celebrations of Holy Communion and baptism to healing services and house blessings. Imagine a deep well of scripture and church tradition and draw from it 'life-giving water' to refresh your faith.

Remember the stories of faith in which water is a powerful symbol. In creation, water was a symbol of the forces of chaos as well as a life-giving force, for it was in creation that the wind of the Holy Spirit swept over the face of the waters and, from a formless void, brought a life-giving order (Genesis 1:1–6). Streams watered the garden of Eden, bringing life in its fullness (2:6), but later, as storms broke, the waters rose and the chaos of flood brought devastation (7:11). Yet still God restored creation: in the story of the flood, perhaps we should recognise as a symbol of the Holy Spirit the dove that brought back a sign of life and peace and then disappeared into the heart of the new creation (8:11–12).

We think of those whose lives are affected by the power of the natural elements and those who make perilous sea journeys. We pray for God's presence in today's waters of chaos, whether literal or symbolic.

We remember the waters parting as the people of Israel fled from slavery towards freedom in the promised land (Exodus 14:21). We think of places today where people are afflicted by 'waters' of oppression, persecution and violence, and we pray that God would part these waters and clear a way for justice, reconciliation and harmony. We think of the countless numbers who have to flee their homelands to find shelter, safety and protection. We pray for the gift of peace.

We also recall Jesus being baptised by John, going down into the waters, rising as if from death to newness and fullness of life, and 'the Spirit of God descending like a dove and alighting on him' (Matthew 3:16). We remember Jesus promising to bring the living water, 'a spring of water gushing up to eternal life' (John 4:14). We pray for the life-giving Spirit to continue to bless our lives.

A spiritual reflection

It was just a drink of water
but it was breaking rules.
It was just small talk at a well
but its content was of abundant life.

A Samaritan woman with her water jar
made her way to the well in the noonday heat,
alone.
Did neighbours shun her?
Did she choose this time to avoid them?
What was her story?
What was her name?
She met Jesus
and he accepted her just as she was,
in her place and her time.

Their chance meeting place was beyond her city,
at a well—
a gift from Jacob,
life-giving for generations.
But here is a better offer:
living water, a spring gushing up for eternal life.

No longer will her mountain, his Jerusalem,
her temple, his temple,
be the way to God.
The living God is released.
God will not be confined.
God calls wherever and whoever
to worship
and know the gift of life-giving, steadfast love.

As she listens intently,
a veil lifts from the drudgery of daily life.
Softly she says,
'I know that the Messiah is coming.
When he comes, he will proclaim all things to us.'
Jesus replies,
'I am he.'

Does time stand still
as belief, hope and reality
rock to and fro?
There is a sense of urgency
as the water jar is left,
and, returning to her city,
she has to ask,
'He cannot be the Messiah,
can he?'

Cooking and meals

Arrange a focus table with a large mixing bowl and a wooden spoon on one side, a chalice and paten on the other, and a cross in the centre.

Welcome and introduction

Our table is set to remind us of meal preparation at home, as well as the meal that Jesus shared with his disciples before he was arrested—a meal that is remembered in services of Holy Communion.

Opening prayers

Introduce the prayer response 'Thanks be to God: Thanks be to God.'

For the fruits of his creation:
Thanks be to God: **Thanks be to God.**

For the opportunity to share a simple cup of tea and a biscuit:
Thanks be to God: **Thanks be to God.**

For Christ taking bread and wine, blessing, breaking and sharing it, so that we might remember his life lived for forgiveness and love:
Thanks be to God: **Thanks be to God.**

Hymn suggestions

- For the fruits of his creation
- Let us break bread together
- Jesus, stand among us

Conversation starters

- What are your favourite meals? What do you like to eat for special meals—for example, birthdays, Christmas or Easter?
- In years gone by, was it traditional for you to eat fish on Fridays?
- Talk about food during World War II and the years afterwards. What were the portions like? Who had what in your family?
- Discuss the present-day need for foodbanks and shelter projects offering meals.
- In the past, only seasonal fruits and vegetables were available in the shops, whereas now, with so much more imported food, almost everything is available all year round. What do you think about this change?
- Do you prefer to shop in local shops or supermarkets? Have you found delivery services available? Does anyone shop online?
- Who taught you to cook? Have you kept your mother's recipe books or didn't she have any?
- When do you eat your main meal?
- Are you vegetarian or restricted to certain foods? Does it make life difficult at times?
- Have you changed your diet as you have become older?
- How do you feel about frozen meals?

- How do you feel about cooking for one, rather than cooking for a family? Are you tempted not to bother?
- What is your experience of hospital food and the assistance that may be needed at meal times in hospital?
- We remember Jesus sharing a meal, the Last Supper, with his disciples. What are your thoughts about Holy Communion? Did you have to attend classes before you were allowed to receive Communion? Do you remember the first time you received Communion?
- Would you like someone to bring Communion to you at home?

Bible reading and introduction

Our reading today takes us to the scene of the Passover in Jerusalem. A room has been prepared where Jesus and his disciples have gathered to celebrate the feast. As we read, we know that this is to be the last supper they will share together, and the words and actions are to become the heart of our worship in services of Holy Communion, connecting us to the Christ.

> While they were eating, he took a loaf of bread, and after blessing it he broke it, gave it to them, and said, 'Take; this is my body.' Then he took a cup, and after giving thanks he gave it to them, and all of them drank from it. He said to them, 'This is my blood of the covenant, which is poured out for many. Truly I tell you, I will never again drink of the fruit of the vine until that day when I drink it new in the kingdom of God.'
>
> MARK 14:22–25

Prayers

Introduce the prayer response 'God, who sustains us: hear our prayer.'

As we pray, we ask God to open our hearts to understand the extraordinary in the ordinary, to remember how scripture reveals the Son of God sharing meals with everyday people, to feel God present in the rhythm of our daily meals.
God, who sustains us: **hear our prayer.**

Lord, we give thanks for the colour and fragrance of food, reminding us of the wonder and provision of creation for the peoples of the world. We enjoy the bright abundance of foods in our shops and supermarkets but we know that many throughout the world and on our doorsteps are hungry. Lord, we pray for those with power in this world to make just and wise decisions, that your people may be fed.
God, who sustains us: **hear our prayer.**

We pray for all who have the responsibility of providing meals, for cooks who work in busy schools, residential homes and hospitals, for all who serve meals and assist in feeding. May patience and love be at the heart of those whose work and service is to give sustenance.
God, who sustains us: **hear our prayer.**

Jesus took bread, blessed and broke it and gave it to his disciples, that they might remember all he had shared and given, and that they might find their way to fullness of life. We give thanks for Jesus, the Christ, the bread of life, who sustains us through the journey of living and dying and offers the gift of eternal life. God, who sustains us: **hear our prayer.**

We say the Lord's Prayer together.

Closing hymn suggestions

- Be still, for the presence of the Lord
- All things bright and beautiful

A blessing

Invite the group to repeat the 'Amen' at the end of each line of the blessing.

May the wonder of God's provision remain in our thoughts. Amen. **Amen**
May the fragrance of Christ's love remain in our hearts. Amen. **Amen**
And may the companionship of the Holy Spirit remain in our souls. Amen. **Amen**

Service of Holy Communion (optional)

Depending on the context, you may wish to offer a short service of Holy Communion, using a service order for home Communion with the reserved sacrament or using denominational patterns of prayer. The following prayers could be said if appropriate.

The peace

The peace we are asked to share is a desire for the very best for each other, the peace that has been made known through Christ. 'God is love, and those who abide in love abide in God, and God abides in them' (1 John 4:16).
The peace of the Lord be with you: **and also with you.**

A prayer of thanksgiving

We look to God who provides for our needs
through the wonder of creation.
We remember
God, who received hospitality from Abram and Sarai;
God, who sent manna from heaven as a people
journeyed from slavery to freedom;
God, whose presence was celebrated
at the feast of kings;
God, at the heart of Passover meals.

We look to God, who sent Jesus to sit and eat,
sharing meals with fieldworkers and fishermen,
women of the kitchen,
the educated and powerful,
the sick and rejected.

When the love of God's Son threatened the powerful,
when his suffering and death were inevitable,
he gathered with his friends for supper
and, filled with grace,
he took bread, blessed and broke it
and gave it to his followers,
saying, 'This is my body and I give it for you.
When you break bread, remember me.'

He took a cup of wine,
blessed it and gave it to them, saying,
'This is my blood, shed for you. When you take the
cup, remember my promises.'

In the ordinary we come to know the extraordinary.

So we pray that we may encounter the love of Christ
in the breaking of bread and the sharing of wine.
We remember Jesus' resurrection and ascension,
where love was released,
and we pray that the Holy Spirit will inspire us
to live and work for acceptance and hospitality,
where fullness of life,
made known in Jesus Christ, will flourish.

Prayer after Communion

We give thanks that, in bread and wine,
we are nourished and blessed with
the love of God,
the hope of Christ
and the companionship of the Holy Spirit. Amen

Closing hymn suggestions

- To God be the glory
- I come with joy

A blessing

May God bless our days with trust and hope,
Christ bless our days with acceptance and hospitality,
and the Holy Spirit bless us with kindness and wisdom.
Amen

Finish with refreshments.

Reflections for the worship leader

The Last Supper: a reflection to kindle your thoughts

My thinking about the Last Supper has undoubtedly been influenced by Godly Play, modern art, liturgy and pastoral, feminist and Black theologies, as well as by individuals.

I thank God for the Godly Play line, 'Jesus said the words of the feast in a way they had never heard before.'[16] These simple words, spoken as a storyteller places figures on a table, hold the impact of that intimate moment between Jesus and his disciples at their last supper together.

What is special about the words of a Holy Communion service for you?

I thank God for Australian artist Margaret Ackland and her modern interpretation of the Last Supper, where men, women and children are shown gathered round the table, facing Jesus. We cannot see his face, yet their expressions and attentiveness to his words speak of his all-embracing love. In the foreground are two almost inconspicuous outlines of people shedding tears, creating a triangle with the figure of Jesus. Does this triangle speak of the Holy Trinity, and of the pain that is to come?

Is there a painting, sculpture or print that speaks to you of the Last Supper?

I thank God for the Revd Dr Stephen Burns, who has been an inspiring liturgical tutor during my ministerial training. I appreciate the breadth, depth and devotion within his priestly ministry, as he creates fully participative worship that never loses sight of our humanity and connects us to the divine in multicoloured words.

Who has shaped your participation in Holy Communion and how has it developed?

I thank God for the depth and difference of theological perspectives, and for insights from Asian theology, particularly R.S. Sugirtharajah's book, *Asian Faces of Jesus*, in which Amaladoss, an Indian Jesuit and theologian, writes, 'Jesus is the Christ, but the Christ is more than Jesus.'[17] These are wonder-filled words that express the humanity, divinity and universality of Jesus and invite conversation in multireligious contexts.

I thank God for Lynne Westfield's book, *Dear Sisters: A womanist practice of hospitality*,[18] which speaks of the gathering of African-American women around tables. As they share meals, they discuss the history (or 'her-story') of incomplete justice and liberation, and the healing nature of community and of hope.

I thank God for the wisdom and creativity of Trevor Dennis, who weaves Old Testament and New Testament theology with issues of the Middle East, refugees and genocide. I love his gift of communicating and challenging through poetry, prose and startling phrases such as 'outrageous forgiveness'.[19]

What nudges and nurtures your reflection on the Last Supper? Is there something from your reflections that you can share with your group with enthusiasm and sincerity?

A spiritual reflection: 'And Jesus took bread...'

Jesus and his followers gathered at a Passover table:
Peter, Judas, John, Andrew.
Mary, Martha, Lazarus?
Bartholomew, Thomas, James.
Mary Magdalene, Susanna, Joanna?
Thaddaeus, or was it Judas (not Iscariot), and Simon.
Mary, mother of Jesus? Matthew, James, Philip.

Who was there?
Who had been invited?
Who just joined in?
Who overheard what he was saying?
Would the Jesus we know have turned people away?

Frown-lined faces of asylum seekers,
etched with anxiety and fear.
Bodies bent with the weight of insecurity,
hesitantly entering unknown territory,
catching a word or maybe two of hymns and prayers
and an invitation to receive bread and wine.
An open invitation? Inclusion or exclusion?
Grace or grief?
Hoops to jump through or the gift of hospitality?

'Come unto me, all that travail and are heavy laden and I will refresh you.'
MATTHEW 11:28, BOOK OF COMMON PRAYER

A service of lament: 'Anger and tears'

The following suggestions for a service of lament will need sensitive adaptation for your particular context and their use may depend upon the depth of your relationship with the group. 'Lament' is a word that has all but slipped from our vocabulary. It is an expression of sorrow or grief that is tucked away and only expressed privately. There have been many indications in recent decades of the need to lament, not only individually but corporately. This need was dramatically visible after the death of Diana, Princess of Wales, in 1997, but these days it is common practice to leave flowers and light candles at the scenes of tragedies. We also see a form of lament in the ritual that developed at Royal Wootton Bassett and continues at RAF Brize Norton, in which family, friends and local people gather for the repatriation of the bodies of fallen soldiers with military flags lowered and flowers cast on the cortège.

The psalmists give a wonderful insight into the process of anger and lament worked out in submission to God. In this submission, people can find release from all that has bound and consumed their hearts and minds. The church is once again recognising the need to lament and finding ways to do it, one illustration being the development of liturgy within the Anglican Church that includes 'Facing Pain: a Service of Lament' in *New Patterns of Worship*. This service offers words of comfort and looks toward hope in the resurrection of Christ, as well as giving an opportunity to lay down the past in prayer and move on to the future in the presence of God.

The service

Arrange a focus table with a cross (not a crucifix), a broken item (for example, a string of beads or a chipped cup) and a basket of pebbles.

Welcome and introduction

The theme for today's service is anger, tears and lament—not easy subjects but emotions that we all experience. There is a broken object on our table to represent something that was precious but is now broken. It can help us to reflect on how we feel when that happens not only to an object but to a person. The cross reminds us of Jesus, his brokenness at his crucifixion, and the emotions felt by those who loved him. Notice that it is an 'empty' cross, reminding us of Jesus' resurrection.

Opening prayers

We meet in the presence of God
who knows our needs,
hears our cries,
feels our pain,
and heals our wounds.[20]

Hymn suggestions

- May the mind of Christ our Saviour
- There is a green hill far away
- Within our darkest night *(Taizé chant)*

Conversation starters

It may be appropriate for the leader to tell a story that focuses on the expression of anger and lament. The following is one that I would choose to use.

Some years ago, the then Dean of Birmingham Cathedral, the Very Revd Gordon Mursell, spoke about the Psalms at The Queen's Foundation, Birmingham. His lecture began dramatically as he slammed his fist on a table and bellowed, 'How long, O Lord, how long?' Mursell reminded us that a cry of despair or a cry for deliverance is frequently heard in the Psalms (for example, Psalm 13; 22; 74; 83), sometimes the cry of an individual and sometimes a communal lament. He went on to say that we can lose the impact of the Psalms when we read them passively.[21]

We need to bring all our emotions to God, including our need to shout and wail, because God (as we understand him in Christ) does not turn away, retaliate or rebuke us. Anger, lament and tears are difficult for us to talk about, but sometimes our experiences, particularly difficult experiences, can help others. It may be helpful to have times when we share such thoughts, knowing that they will remain confidential, and times when we listen to other people's laments without passing judgement.

- What kinds of things have made you angry?
- Have there been experiences at school or work that have angered you?
- Do local issues ever anger you—perhaps a supermarket development, cuts to bus services or litter on the streets?
- Do you feel the same about national and international issues, such as wars in foreign countries, asylum seekers, economic migrants or the market economy?
- Are you angered by misuse of power and corruption, leading to hunger, poverty and helplessness?
- Have you ever encountered racism? How did it make you feel?
- Abuse in many different contexts, including abuse of children and vulnerable adults, has a high profile. Do you feel that issues are being properly addressed?
- You may not wish to share your experience, but have you experienced despair or helplessness when someone was in pain, or have you felt anger at illness and death?
- Have you encountered unkind attitudes because of your ageing or frailty?

Bible readings

Read the following psalm (Psalm 13) as a dramatic monologue.

How long, O Lord? Will you forget me for ever?
How long will you hide your face from me?
How long must I bear pain in my soul,
and have sorrow in my heart all day long?
How long shall my enemy be exalted over me?

Consider and answer me, O Lord my God!
Give light to my eyes, or I will sleep the sleep of death,

and my enemy will say, 'I have prevailed';
my foes will rejoice because I am shaken.

But I trusted in your steadfast love;
my heart shall rejoice in your salvation.
I will sing to the Lord,
because he has dealt bountifully with me.

If we move to the New Testament, we glimpse Jesus' righteous anger, tears and lament in the Gospels. Luke's Gospel describes Jesus weeping over Jerusalem as he approaches the city, just days before the Last Supper (Luke 19:41). Jesus then enters the temple, where his anger rises at the sight of the marketplace scene in which money is exchanged for sacrificial offerings sold at inflated prices (v. 45). In John's Gospel, his anger is described in even more physical terms as he drives out the merchants and money changers with a whip made of cords (John 2:15). I often wonder whether Jesus' tone of voice changed as he spoke the words from Isaiah, 'It is written, "My house shall be a house of prayer"; but you have made it a den of robbers' (Luke 19:46). Was there despair, grief and yearning in his tone? Was this, for him, a moment of lament?

As he came near and saw the city, he wept over it, saying, 'If you, even you, had only recognised on this day the things that make for peace! But now they are hidden from your eyes. Indeed, the days will come upon you, when your enemies will set up ramparts around you and surround you, and hem you in on every side. They will crush you to the ground, you and your children within you, and they will not leave within you one stone upon another; because you did not recognise the time of your visitation from God.'

Then he entered the temple and began to drive out those who were selling things there; and he said, 'It is written, "My house shall be a house of prayer"; but you have made it a den of robbers.'

Every day he was teaching in the temple. The chief priests, the scribes, and the leaders of the people kept looking for a way to kill him; but they did not find anything they could do, for all the people were spellbound by what they heard.
LUKE 19:41–48

Prayers

Offer people a stone or pebble to hold throughout these prayers.

We bring to God all that has made us angry—major issues in which we feel so powerless.

We bring the times when we have felt anger because systems we trusted have failed; times when care or a diagnosis has not been given in the way we would have hoped; times when we have felt broken or those close to us have been broken by circumstances.

We bring what may seem like small or inevitable changes in our own lives that we struggle with—bodies that no longer do what we would like them to, or minds that do not always understand what is happening in this age of fast-changing technology. We lament that the world moves on from where we were, to unknown territory.

There are times, Lord, when we would like to hurl this stone, as a symbol of our anger and frustration, into an abyss. 'But you are the same Lord, whose nature is always to have mercy.'[22] You know our needs, you hear our cry, and you say, 'Come unto me, all ye that labour and are heavy laden, and I will give you rest' (Matthew 11:28, KJV).

As we hold on to our stone, we are reminded that you are our rock. You shape, mould and hold us, no matter where we are or how we feel. You will not desert us and, when we are too tired to pray, too anxious to feel your presence, you are there, an invisible cradle of our living and dying.

'The steadfast love of the Lord never ceases, his mercies never come to an end; they are new every morning; great is your faithfulness' (Lamentations 3:22–23).

We say the Lord's Prayer together.

Closing hymn suggestions

- Spirit of the living God
- O God, our help in ages past

A blessing

May the peace of God,
which passes all understanding,
keep our hearts and minds
in the knowledge and love of God,
and of his Son Jesus Christ our Lord;
and the blessing of God almighty,
the Father, the Son, and the Holy Spirit,
be among us and remain with us always. Amen[23]

Reflections for the worship leader

A biblical reflection

Spend some time with the tears of Psalm 137:1:

By the rivers of Babylon—
there we sat down and there we wept
when we remembered Zion.

These could be words for those who are exiled from life by ageing—weeping for home, weeping for lost loved ones, weeping for a familiar way of life.

Did Jesus feel in exile as he wept for Jerusalem? Did he weep for days at the lakeside, where he saw people's longing and need? Did he remember boat trips in storms, and weep for the disciples who needed to trust in God? Did he weep for those who rejected his teaching, for those who whispered and plotted? Did he remember John the Baptist's untimely brutal death and face the reality of his own death?

As he came near and saw the city, he wept over it, saying, 'If you, even you, had only recognised on this day the things that make for peace! But now they are hidden from your eyes' (Luke 19:41–42).

Tears for Jerusalem turned to anger in the temple, where so many guardians of the faith had created systems that held people captive to rituals, while the holy hierarchy lived in fear of losing power and authority. Jesus still yearned for people to understand God's purposes and the all-embracing love of the Holy One. Tears turned to anger, and then anger to lament.

And he said, 'It is written, "My house shall be a house of prayer"; but you have made it a den of robbers' (Luke 19:46).

A spiritual reflection

An early morning news bulletin wakens us from sleep;
headlines break into our semi-consciousness.
An efficient newsreading voice informs
a million listeners:
'Violence in the Middle East escalated overnight,
with large numbers of casualties, the death toll rising.'

How long, O Lord?

It could be any century, BC or AD.
It is right now.

How long, O Lord?

We are, by all accounts,
within 'six degrees of separation' from one another.
Social networking makes it, perhaps, only four degrees.

Just four links of a chain away—
a friend of a friend of a friend of a friend—
from someone who may never have known
a day of peace,
a day of life in its fullness.
And yet we feel so utterly helpless!

How long, O Lord?

How many steps are we from you, O Lord?
Only one, for you have called us friends—
and not even that one step,
for you are within and around and beyond.
'You have searched me and known me' (Psalm 139:1).
You are there;
your peace and your love are there.

As I take 'the wings of the morning' (Psalm 139:9)
into my places of encounter,
help me to find a word
that speaks of the hope and faith
I have in the love of Christ
to a friend who is a friend of a friend of a friend...

A service of healing: 'Fragile bones'

As in the service of anger and tears, a good relationship between the worship leader and group is essential here. The conversation starters fall into two parts, with the second part needing careful consideration before use.

The service

Arrange a focus table with an upturned clay pot (broken on one side), a candle inside the pot, and a cross. (You may be able to find an appropriate symbolic cross—for example, one made of materials from a derelict church, a cross of nails, a brightly coloured Salvadoran cross expressing belief and hope from the suffering people of El Salvador, or a crucifix.)

Welcome and introduction

The broken clay pot on our table has a candle inside as a symbol of the Christ-light within us. I have placed it so that, although you cannot see the light within, you know it is there. When I turn the pot to show its broken side, the light shines, symbolising all that was revealed through Christ's death and resurrection.[24]

Opening prayers

Read or sing Psalm 23.

The Lord is my shepherd, I shall not want.
He makes me lie down in green pastures;
he leads me beside still waters;
he restores my soul.
He leads me in right paths
for his name's sake.

Even though I walk through the darkest valley,
I fear no evil;
for you are with me;
your rod and your staff—
they comfort me.

You prepare a table before me
in the presence of my enemies;
you anoint my head with oil;
my cup overflows.
Surely goodness and mercy shall follow me
all the days of my life,
and I shall dwell in the house of the Lord
my whole life long.

Conversation starters (Part 1)

- How are the aches and pains of life? On a scale of 1 to 10, how do you feel today?
- Have you or someone close to you had experience of health issues, from hip or knee operations to feeling really down-hearted?

- What is the most frustrating or difficult thing about ageing? What is good about it?
- The diagnosis of a condition is rarely an easy moment for yourself or for family or friends. If you have experienced this, what helped or could have helped you? What didn't help?
- What do you think about miraculous healing? What do you understand by it?
- Have you ever met someone or heard a story about healing that seemed miraculous?
- Have you had any experience of healing services or prayer meetings? Were they helpful or not?
- What do you think about the healing stories in the Gospels? (It may be helpful to give an example—perhaps the healing of the paralysed man in Luke 5:17–26.) Do you have any comments or questions about them?

Conversation starters (Part 2)

It may be that members of the group mention dying as a kind of healing, which may provide a window into further discussion. The following questions offer some ideas for the development of that discussion, if it is appropriate.

- Have you ever journeyed with someone through their dying? What are your experiences of seeing the end of life in hospitals, homes or hospices? Some places have 'end of life plans': what do you think about that?
- Do you want to share any comments, thoughts or experiences on an untimely, unexpected or sudden death?
- Does anyone ever talk to you about your own dying?
- How do you feel about a priest, minister or chaplain being a part of the process of dying? Is there anything you would

like them to do in particular? Would the opportunity for confession, commending yourself to God, anointing or Communion be helpful?
- What do you most want to share with others?
- What seems clearer to you at this point of your life?

Bible reading and introduction

Sometimes it is within our own weakness and brokenness that we feel the presence of Christ, and sometimes we may simply feel his absence and have to trust in his presence. Paul, in his second letter to the Corinthians, writes about his great trust in Christ, and the hope that Paul offers has travelled down the centuries to speak to us today.

> For it is the God who said, 'Let light shine out of darkness', who has shone in our hearts to give the light of the knowledge of the glory of God in the face of Jesus Christ. But we have this treasure in clay jars, so that it may be made clear that this extraordinary power belongs to God and does not come from us. We are afflicted in every way, but not crushed; perplexed, but not driven to despair; persecuted, but not forsaken; struck down, but not destroyed; always carrying in the body the death of Jesus, so that the life of Jesus may also be made visible in our bodies. For while we live, we are always being given up to death for Jesus' sake, so that the life of Jesus may be made visible in our mortal flesh. So death is at work in us, but life in you.
> 2 CORINTHIANS 4:6–12

Prayers

Ask for prayer requests. Introduce the prayer response, 'God, who knows our needs: hear our prayer.'

We come in prayer as individuals who are a part of the worldwide communities of faith. We give thanks that, no matter how broken the church is, or how fragile are our communities, the grace of Christ is present.
God, who knows our needs: **hear our prayer.**

We come in prayer for our broken world, torn apart by war and poverty. We so often feel lost for words, powerless and without hope as we see and hear of tragedies beyond our understanding. We trust, O Lord, that you are the God of mercy, and pray that your will may be done and your kingdom come.
God, who knows our needs: **hear our prayer.**

We come in prayer for our own particular circumstances, for strength for our own fragile bones, for all that is fragile in our lives. In times when we have no peace within ourselves and our bodily strength fades, may our spiritual strength be nourished by the presence of God. May we trust and know that in our most difficult moments your love will never desert us.
God, who knows our needs: **hear our prayer.**

We remember the apostle Paul's words: 'I am convinced that neither death, nor life, nor angels, nor rulers, nor things present, nor things to come, nor powers, nor height, nor depth, nor anything else in all creation, will be able to separate us from the love of God in Christ Jesus our Lord' (Romans 8:38–39).

Let us say together the Lord's Prayer.

Closing hymn suggestions

- I heard the voice of Jesus say
- Just as I am
- Be still and know that I am God

A blessing

Introduce the prayer response, 'God bless us: God bless us.'

In our aches and pains, God bless us: **God bless us.**
In our highs and lows, God bless us: **God bless us.**
In our living and dying, God bless us: **God bless us.**
And may we be blessed with the knowledge of God's love for us through our Saviour, Jesus Christ. Amen

Take time for reflection while quiet music plays (for example, Elgar's 'Nimrod' from the Enigma Variations, *or 'Air on a G string' by J.S. Bach.*

Finish with refreshments.

Reflections for the worship leader

A biblical reflection

Paul's words in 2 Corinthians 4:6–12 have much to say to us as our bodies become frail. It is a reading that speaks of the treasure of the light of Christ, and we hold this treasure in our individual bodies, which Paul describes as clay jars. Before his conversion, Paul (then known as Saul) was a Pharisee, intent on persecuting the early disciples, but after his conversion he worked tirelessly as an apostle of Christ. His knowledge of Hebrew scripture would have been profound, as he had been educated by Gamaliel, a leading authority in the Sanhedrin, and his letters frequently made connections with the images and themes of the prophets.

The following two quotations from the Old Testament add to Paul's image of our bodies as clay jars. As Isaiah laments the sinful nature of God's people and the apparent absence of God, he says, 'Yet, O Lord, you are our Father; we are the clay, and you are our potter; we are all the work of your hand' (Isaiah 64:8). Then, in Jeremiah we find the allegory of the potter, illustrating God's creation and recreation of good in the midst of destruction:

> *The word that came to Jeremiah from the Lord: 'Come, go down to the potter's house, and there I will let you hear my words.' So I went down to the potter's house, and there he was working at his wheel. The vessel he was making of clay was spoiled in the potter's hand, and he reworked it into another vessel, as seemed good to him (Jeremiah 18:1–4).*

We often feel rather like clay jars in need of reworking. Life makes cracks and chips in us, and we end up feeling vulnerable, even broken. However, although we would not choose to be frail or broken, we may find that all kinds of truths become visible as a result. Then there is the potential for God to remake us.

Jesus would be truly visible to his followers as the Christ only after his crucifixion and resurrection. Only through death could his life-light be truly known.

A spiritual reflection

Beyond
wrinkles,
bright shining or glazed lost eyes,
arthritic joints and wasting limbs,
the odours of incontinence
and every conceivable complaint and disease,
there is an individual story.

Advice abounds for visits to elderly folk:
'Take a memory book, grapes, music; a short stay;
Just chat.'
Another says,
'The most important thing is that you are there.
Read a poem or psalm; take a well-loved book.'
Or some say,
'Don't be afraid of sharing silence.'
Advice rooted in individual experience.

We may sit long in a car park,
willing ourselves to cross the threshold
of a home or hospital.
We may race in, anxious for every moment,
struggle to leave,
and then need to debrief or be alone and in silence.
The process is individual.
But no matter how different each experience,
the visitor needs to be told,
'It is OK; you are doing fine.'
Then peace stands a chance,
and healing of our own wounds can happen.

You are doing fine.

'All shall be well, and all shall be well, and all manner of thing shall be well' (Julian of Norwich).[25]

A closing liturgy: 'Holy journeying'

The following liturgy is a development of a closing service held for the Women's Fellowship Group that met at St Peter's Church, Hall Green, Birmingham. The service offered an opportunity to give thanks to God for the life of the group, remembering much of what had been shared and looking to the future. The gathering included a few friends and relatives of the group members, plus clergy and speakers who had participated in the monthly devotional and fortnightly meetings over many years.

Informal conversation before the service briefly recapped some of the themes explored in previous months before we moved into the liturgy with music to mark the beginning of worship and reflection. On this occasion we used a service sheet in large print, with members of the fellowship saying the words in bold. The group's favourite hymns featured as part of the service.

This liturgy could be used for other times of closure (for example, leaving a family home for different accommodation) by adapting prayers, adjusting the 'Remembering' and 'Looking to the future' sections, and considering appropriate verses of scripture for the context.

The service

Arrange a focus table with a dish holding a large candle surrounded by five smaller candles and pebbles.

Welcome and introduction

We meet in the name of God, known in Christ and the Holy Spirit.

Hymn

- The old rugged cross *(or another favourite)*

Opening responses

Print out the following prayer, with the responses in bold for the group to say together.

God of time that has gone before us,
we give thanks that you were there
when we had lost hope,
and there when all was well.
God of our years, we thank you.

God of time that is to come,
we have heard your words:
'The steadfast love of the Lord never ceases,
his mercies never come to an end;
they are new every morning,
great is your faithfulness' (Lamentations 3:22–23).
We place our trust for the future in you.
God of this moment,
the time of the closure of this group,
we come with our memories and prayers.

Hymn

- O God, our help in ages past

Remembering

Draw people's attention to the dish of candles and pebbles. Light the large candle first and allow time for memories to be spoken aloud or recalled silently, as the smaller candles are lit. Again, the prayer can be printed out, with responses in bold.

We light the large candle
to remind us of the light of God,
as Father, Son and Holy Spirit.
We light a candle for this group,
a candle for those who have visited as speakers,
a candle for friends and family,
a candle for members who have died
and a candle for the churches
of which members have been a part
throughout their lives.

The pebbles represent the smoothness of good times
and the roughness and sharpness of difficult times.
As others who have gone before
laid down what had become familiar and safe,
so we let go of this group,
treasuring the fellowship
and taking our prayers as we go.

As others who left familiar patterns of life,
stepping into an unknown future,
so we look to journey
with the pattern of God's promise and love.

As others have left activity behind
and live quietly in your presence,
may we live aware of your love.

Hymn

- Just as I am

Bible reading

During the service at St Peter's, Hall Green, the Liturgy of the Word began with Genesis 12:1–3. The Godly Play story of Abram and Sarai was told, with the emphasis that wherever Abram and Sarai made their home, they prayed their thanks to God.

If you or your group are not familiar with Godly Play, it would be more appropriate to read or tell the story of Abram and Sarai, briefly describing their journeys and focusing on the fact that God was present in their journeying.

Looking to the future

Is there a way you can keep in touch with one another, even though the group is closing? What sort of support would you like in your continuing journey in faith?

Discuss how arrangements can be made for visits from members of the church for fellowship, prayer and home Communion. Remind the group that prayer is available for individuals through prayer groups within the church, prayer partners and Sunday intercessions. (Make contact lists available.)

The Peace

Jesus said, 'Peace I leave with you; my peace I give to you' (John 14:27).

The peace of the Lord be always with you.
And also with you.

We offer one another a sign of peace.

Where mobility is difficult, suggest that people simply offer a smile and a wave rather than moving around to give the sign of peace.

Hymn

- Be still, for the presence of the Lord

Prayers

Introduce the prayer response from Common Worship, *'Lord, hear us: Lord, graciously hear us.'*

We bring to God all that we are:
'Just as I am, though tossed about
With many a conflict, many a doubt,
fightings and fears within, without,
O Lamb of God, I come.'[26]
Lord, hear us: **Lord, graciously hear us.**

We come knowing that God is always
the midwife of our lives.
In times when all things are uncertain,
God's will is that we might have fullness of life—
life that, even in frailty, is full
of the all-encompassing love of God.
Lord, hear us: **Lord, graciously hear us.**

We give thanks for the many gifts with which God has blessed us with *[name some of the gifts of the group: listening, making refreshments, being a good companion, being honest, defusing difficult situations]*.
Lord, hear us: **Lord, graciously hear us.**

We give thanks for the creative presence
of God in our lives,
weaving patterns of love in encounters,
phone calls and cards.
Lord, hear us: **Lord, graciously hear us.**

We give thanks for all we have given
and received at this group,
and we look to the future,
trusting in your hope and love
that were seen, above all, in Christ our Saviour.

'Just as I am, of that free love
the breadth, length, depth and height to prove,
here for a season, then above,
O Lamb of God, I come.'

We say the Lord's Prayer together.

We rest in the power of God's love
for each of us and all of us.
and together pray the Grace:
The grace of our Lord Jesus Christ, and the love of God, and the fellowship of the Holy Spirit, be with us all evermore. Amen.

Pray as you snuff out the candles:

As we blow the candles out, we no longer see the light of God, but, just as the smoke rises and mingles among us, so the light of God goes with us.

Hymn

- Abide with me

A blessing

May the peace of God,
which passes all understanding,
keep our hearts and minds
in the knowledge and love of God,
and of his Son Jesus Christ our Lord:
and the blessing of God Almighty
the Father, the Son and the Holy Spirit,
be among us and remain with us always. Amen

Refreshments

It would be lovely if special refreshments were provided by members of the church to mark this significant occasion, perhaps even including a bottle of champagne.

Reflections for the worship leader

A biblical reflection

The story of Abram and Sarai was well received at the closing service for the St Peter's fellowship group. It offered much food for reflection: how does it feel to leave beautiful cities, homes or churches where there has been a sense of reasonable security, where a person knows and is known?

The story has particular significance for the 'Windrush generation' (people who emigrated from the Caribbean to Britain in 1948 on the SS *Empire Windrush*, and subsequent immigrants during that era), and for recent refugees and asylum seekers who find themselves ageing in a 'strange land', often separated from family and long-term friends.

Although the events of Genesis 12:10–20, which took place in Egypt, are not a focus in this context, I always think of Abram's behaviour towards Sarai as shameful. Abram feared he might be killed if it was known that Sarai was his wife, so, without thought for her safety, he asked her to lie about her identity and say that she was his sister. The dragons of fear can never be underestimated, particularly when a person is feeling vulnerable. I wonder how well we understand the dragons of fear for elderly people, and whether we create opportunities for them to name those fears.

Many places in scripture speak about journeying and offer a means for reflection with our 'sages'. I think of David and the honour and integrity he showed on his life journey. For example, he could easily have killed Saul in the cave at En-gedi (1 Samuel 24:1–7) but chose not to do so, because Saul was the Lord's anointed. However, as anointed king over a united Israel and Judah, his conduct concerning Uriah and Bathsheba was an abuse of his power (2 Samuel 11:2–15). He turned from the goodness and authority of God, only to realise later that he had separated himself from God's presence. Journeys do not often come as easy package trips.

Another story that is appropriate for a closing service is Luke's account of the disciples on the Emmaus road (Luke 24:13–35). The travellers were so immersed in discussing

Jesus, their prophet 'mighty in deed and word before God' (v. 19), yet condemned to death, that when someone joined them on their journey, they could not see who it was. They thought that the time of Jesus was over, but they were about to see, as bread was taken, blessed, broken and shared, that the eternal time of Christ had begun. Journeying into dependent living may feel like travelling on a lonely Emmaus road, and an assurance of the presence of Christ may be necessary.

A spiritual reflection

Closings as we age are sometimes a relief,
a time of celebration,
a time of mourning.
Closings may create an aching gap
in time and companionship.
Closings open the door to an unknown future.

Will the eyes of community
be so distracted by the daily round of busyness
that time will slip away
and connections be lost
or will the heart of community
encompass our solitary sages,
and all be unexpectedly enriched
by sharing the gift of ageing?

The substance of small talk

Small talk is heard in countless places, on bus journeys and at banquets, between neighbours and strangers, before and after church services (the unwritten rule of sacred silence before a service being challenged by those who feel that the small talk of daily life is a vital ingredient in fellowship and worship). The conversation starters in each liturgy in this book could be described as small talk. They are everyday subjects of seemingly little importance, yet they unlock significant conversation and give shape and substance to worship.

The Gospels could hardly be described as small talk—every word counts, giving insight into the person of Jesus and the purposes of God—but Jesus used imagery that was the stuff of small talk, such as water, seeds, weeds and salt. Matthew gives us a good example: 'You are the salt of the earth; but if salt has lost its taste, how can its saltiness be restored? It is no longer good for anything, but is thrown out and trampled underfoot' (Matthew 5:13). Dare we imagine the chatter from some quarters when his words were recalled? 'Salt! I'll give him salt! Does he have any idea about the price? I reckon Eliud is on the make—I saw him with a flagon of oil. How could he afford that? If you ask me, he's as bad as some of the other traders, mixing salt with all sorts of stuff, making our lives even more of a misery!'

Sometimes small talk can be so near and yet so far from the greater truth. In the chatter, the metaphors of faith and the images of the kingdom of God may not have been immediately understood but they were ready to be discovered in further discussion after Jesus' death and resurrection. The one who opens the door to that discussion is playing a significant role.

The disciples asked many questions of Jesus, genuinely failing to understand what he was imparting. I wonder if Jesus created such vivid imagery in his parables so that, when minds wandered, his message would be easy to picture. At the end of the parable of the sower, for example, I imagine Jesus loudly declaring—even shouting, but with a twinkle in his eye—'Let anyone with ears to hear listen!' (Luke 8:8). His words are a reminder to us all to listen with care to what is said and unsaid, to reflect, respond and, in so doing, create the ground where the word will flourish.

We live in a society that has been intent on defining and enforcing 'normality'. I say 'has been' because boundaries are slowly beginning to be removed in areas of gender, sexuality, ethnic origins and disabilities. However, the focus on well-being, combating or denying physical or mental decline—particularly in the natural process of ageing—sometimes seems like a state of denial. A phrase emerged from discussion among my student group at theological college: 'the tyranny of normality'. It spoke of the power of 'normality' to signpost only that which is strong, and to leave weakness and vulnerability at the side of the road. When dependent living creates isolation from 'normality' and separates Christians from their community, what is the community's response?

Is this issue a priority? What are the limitations of human resources? There are no easy answers. Generalisations are inadequate and so the question remains: how can the church community better prepare individuals for their faith journey in later years and particularly in the transition time from independence to dependence?

There is much to discover and, as I personally move towards being labelled as an 'older adult', I look to words that may become spiritual companions. John 15:1–5 has always had great significance for me throughout the decades of life. Now, as I observe the 'pruning' that sages encounter—decluttering homes, downsizing, moving to assisted accommodation and sometimes to specialist nursing care—the Word that was there in the beginning, there in death, made alive in resurrection, and remains our eternal Word—rings out from this passage and offers much comfort for the times of transition.

I am the true vine, and my Father is the vine-grower. He removes every branch in me that bears no fruit. Every branch that bears fruit he prunes to make it bear more fruit. You have already been cleansed by the word that I have spoken to you. Abide in me as I abide in you. Just as the branch cannot bear fruit by itself unless it abides in the vine, neither can you unless you abide in me. I am the vine, you are the branches. Those who abide in me and I in them bear much fruit, because apart from me you can do nothing.

JOHN 15:1–5

Notes

1 Theologians define 'sages' in more detail. For example, 'A sage is one who has done the inner work necessary to act in the world with pure being, transcendence of the personal self, and direct connection with the sacred. Sages also manifest cognitive, emotional and contemplative wisdom' (Robert C. Atchley, *Spirituality and Aging* (Johns Hopkins University Press, 2009), p. 76.

2 Penelope Wilcock, 'The caged bird: thoughts on the challenge of living with a stroke', in Albert Jewell (ed.), *Ageing, Spirituality and Well-being* (Jessica Kingsley, 2003), ch. 4.

3 James Woodward, *Valuing Age* (SPCK, 2008).

4 Kate Read, 'What is dementia?' in James Woodward (ed.), *Between Remembering and Forgetting: The spiritual dimensions of dementia* (Mowbray, 2010), ch. 1.

5 Trevor Dennis, *Looking God in the Eye: Encountering God in Genesis* (SPCK, 1998), p. 7.

6 Peter Atkins, *Memory and Liturgy: The place of memory in the composition and practice of liturgy* (Ashgate, 2003), p. 67.

7 'O God, make the door of this house wide enough to receive all who need human love and fellowship and a heavenly Father's care; and narrow enough to shut out all envy, pride and hate. Make its threshold smooth enough to be no stumbling block to children or to straying feet, but rugged enough to turn back the tempter's power; make it a gateway to thine eternal kingdom' (Thomas Ken, 1637–1711). The St Peter's Women's Fellowship adapted Thomas Ken's prayer and prayed it from memory at their meetings.

8 Graeme Smith and Will Adam, 'Hidden ecumenism' in *Theology* Vol. C111, No. 816 (November 2000), p. 412.

9 Malcolm Goldsmith, *In a Strange Land...: People with dementia and the local church* (4M, 2004), p. 94.

10 From the Irish hymn, 'Be thou my vision', English translation by Eleanor Hull (1912).

11 A series of videos with footage from scientists who monitored the Soufrière Hills in Montserrat before, during and after the fatal eruption in 1997. Includes interviews with local people. Video by David Lea, Living Letters Ministries, Box 246, Plymouth, Montserrat, Leeward islands, British West Indies.
12 John Hull, *Touching the Rock: An experience of blindness* (Arrow, 1990).
13 Hull, *Touching the Rock*, p. 49.
14 From the hymn 'O thou who camest from above' by Charles Wesley (1707–88).
15 *Sanctuary: By Celtic Waters*, Samuel Reid (Ashmore Audio/Willow Productions, 1998).
16 Sonja M. Stewart and Jerome Berryman, *Young Children and Worship* (Westminster John Knox, 2011), p. 190.
17 Michael Amaladoss, 'The pluralism of religions and the significance of Christ' in R.S. Sugirtharajah (ed.), *Asian Faces of Jesus* (SCM Press, 2013), p. 95.
18 N. Lynne Westfield, *Dear Sisters: A womanist practice of hospitality*, (Pilgrim Press, 2001).
19 Trevor Dennis, *God Treads Softly Here* (SPCK, 2004), p. 94.
20 Opening prayer from 'Facing Pain: a service of lament', *New Patterns for Worship* (Church House Publishing, 2008).
21 Gordon Mursell, 'The place of lament in Christian spirituality' (lecture at The Queen's Foundation, 23 January 2005).
22 'Prayer of humble access', *Common Worship: Services and Prayers for the Church of England.*
23 'The peace of God', *Common Worship: Services and Prayers for the Church of England.*
24 From an idea created by Revd Mark Townsend for retreats and described in *The Gospel of Falling Down: The beauty of failure, in an age of success* (O Books, 2007). Adapted with author's permission.
25 Julian of Norwich, in Robert Llewelyn (ed.), *Enfolded in Love: Daily readings with Julian of Norwich* (DLT, 2004), p. 15.
26 'Just as I am, without one plea' by Charlotte Elliot (1789–1871).

The Gift of Years is BRF's newest initiative, which we started to develop in 2014. In recent years, Debbie Thrower (former BBC and ITV journalist and presenter) has developed a highly effective model for community-based 'Anna Chaplaincy' to older people in Alton, Hampshire. BRF embraced the 'Anna Chaplain' model as the centrepiece of a new ministry, The Gift of Years, whose vision is 'resourcing the spiritual journey of older people'. Through this we are seeking both to resource older people themselves and also to resource ministry among older people, wherever they may be—in congregations, in residential care, in their own homes and in the community.

To explore this ministry, discover resources and get involved, please visit www.thegiftofyears.org.uk.